THE NEW LEFT AND THE ORIGINS
OF THE COLD WAR

ROBERT
JAMES
MADDOX

The New Left
and the Origins of
the Cold War

PRINCETON

UNIVERSITY

PRESS

PRINCETON

N.J.

For Barbara

CONTENTS

ACKNOWLEDGMENTS

I AM indebted to a number of scholars for having taken the time to read portions of this manuscript during its preparation. Some will recognize their own suggestions. I am especially grateful to the late Herbert Feis for having persuaded me to put aside another project temporarily in order to complete this work. Three colleagues, Dick Garner, Gerry Eggert, and George Enteen, demonstrated both patience and endurance as I told them far more than they ever wished to know about the origins of the Cold War.

The Liberal Arts Central Fund for Research and the Slavic Language and Area Center at the Pennsylvania State University aided me in preparing the manuscript. Grateful acknowledgment is also made for permission to reprint in revised form materials that were first published as: "Cold War Revisionism: Abusing History," *Freedom at Issue* (September-October 1972), 3-6, 16-19; and "Atomic Diplomacy: A Study in Creative Writing," *Journal of American History* (March 1973).

November 1972   RJM

THE NEW LEFT AND THE ORIGINS

OF THE COLD WAR

INTRODUCTION

I N recent years the most controversial issue in American diplomatic history has been the origins of the Cold War. As more and more people have come to reexamine their assumptions about present U.S. foreign policies, they have called into question the roots of those policies. How did the Cold War begin? Who or what was responsible? Could it have been avoided? Was it a temporary condition created by a combination of individual personalities and historical factors, or did it represent the clash of fundamentally irreconcilable systems? Beginning earlier, but attracting wide attention since the mid-1960's, a number of scholars more or less identified with the New Left have challenged the conventional, or "orthodox," answers to these questions. Although by no means monolithic in their own interpretations, the New Left revisionists collectively have mounted a formidable attack on the conventional wisdom. And they have done so in such a way as to focus attention on the very nature of the American system itself, as well as its foreign policy.

The orthodox explanation of the how the Cold War began has been stated most succinctly by Arthur Schlesinger, jr.: it was "the brave and essential response of free men to communist aggression" at the close of World War II. Regardless of what we know now or might learn in the future about Russian intentions then, according to this view, American leaders at the time reacted defensively against what they could only consider to be systematic violations of wartime agreements. Orthodox scholars have differed in what they see as the causes of Soviet behavior, assigning various weights to factors such as traditional Russian foreign policy goals, the dynamics of the Soviet system, and Josef Stalin's personal characteristics. They have also differed over the appropriateness of the American response. All of them, however, agree in attributing the origins of the struggle to Soviet initiatives.

Although the revisionists disagree among themselves on a wide range of specific issues—the role of the atomic bomb in American diplomacy, for instance—they tend to divide into two recognizable groups. The "soft" revisionists place far more emphasis upon individuals than they do on the nature of institutions or systems. They see a sharp break between the foreign policies of Franklin D. Roosevelt and Harry S Truman, and place responsibility for the Cold War on Truman and the men around him. Truman, according to this view, broke apart a functioning coalition soon after he took office. To the "soft" revisionists, therefore, the Cold War came about because of the failure of American statesmanship.

The "hard" revisionists raise more fundamental issues. To these scholars the Cold War was the inevitable result of the American system as it developed over the years. Based upon what American leaders perceived as the need for continuous economic expansion abroad, the corporate structure itself shaped foreign policies. Whatever personal differences existed among individuals, all American policymakers were dedicated to creating an American-dominated world order which would permit the system to expand unhindered. When Russia refused to acquiesce in

4

American world hegemony, particularly in Eastern Europe, she perforce came to be defined as the enemy. Although the "hard" revisionists themselves emphasize the events of World War II and its immediate aftermath, they see this era merely as a phase—the latest being the American intervention in Vietnam—of the ongoing struggle between a conservative capitalist order and world revolution. They reject completely the notion that American–Russian relations would have evolved very differently had F.D.R. lived, or had someone other than Truman taken his place.

Most of the revisionists frankly proclaim that they conceive of their work as a tool for change. The "softs" wish to influence present policy by demonstrating past errors, the "hards" to show the need for a radical restructuring of the existing system. They reject the notion of "objective" history, arguing that all too often that term has been used to describe what in fact were scholarly rationalizations for official policies. "It is past time, the revisionists believe," one scholar has written, "for the admission that for American historians history begins and ends with ideology."[1] The historian's job, therefore, is to create a version of the past which can be used to help achieve the goals his ideological preferences dictate.

Some of the revisionists, without denying the influence of ideology, have also questioned the integrity of their orthodox colleagues. William Appleman Williams, for instance, refers to two approaches one can take toward his

[1] Walter LaFeber, "War: Cold," *Cornell Alumni News* (October 1968), reprinted in James V. Compton (ed.), *America and the Origins of the Cold War* (Boston: Houghton Mifflin, 1972), 175-186.

INTRODUCTION

discipline. The first "defines history as a stockpile of facts to be requisitioned on the basis of what is needed to prove a conclusion decided upon in advance." The other is "to consider history as a way of learning, of mustering the intellectual and moral courage to acknowledge the facts as they exist without tampering with them."[2] Since he identifies the second approach as his own, it must be the orthodox scholars who have refused to "acknowledge the facts as they exist without tampering with them." David Horowitz has been even more explicit. Writing ominously of "a propagandistic view of the history of the post-war years" and of "accepted versions originating in Washington," he accuses orthodox scholars of consciously promoting "the State Department line."[3] The conclusion is inescapable: only the revisionists possess sufficient courage to reveal truths which must have been obvious to even the most dull-witted orthodox scholar.

Orthodox historians have responded, though without the ardor one might expect given the issues involved and the allegations made. Possibly reflecting their own doubts about previously held assumptions, most have shown far greater tolerance toward their New Left critics than the latter have granted them. Only very recently have there appeared the kinds of sophisticated analyses of revisionist works that the significance of the questions raised clearly warrants. And it is interesting to note that most of these have been written by younger men who bear no

[2] William Appleman Williams, *The Tragedy of American Diplomacy* (rev. and enl. edn., New York: Dell, 1962), 207.

[3] David Horowitz, *The Free World Colossus: A Critique of American Foreign Policy in The Cold War* (rev. edn., New York: Hill and Wang, 1971), 5, 7.

6

onus of having been Cold War "warriors," rather than by those whose once-standard accounts have been called into question.

Critical examinations of revisionism have ranged from the broadest theoretical considerations of the nature of capitalism and its institutions to matters of selecting and emphasizing evidence.[4] Only a few of the more obvious complaints can be mentioned here. Revisionists almost always employ a double-standard: Russia's actions are justified or explained by reference to national security or *Realpolitik*, Western actions are measured against some high ideal and found wanting. This approach extends even to the texture of their prose. One revisionist, writing about the suppression of leftist factions in Greece, could scarcely contain his outrage. There was, he wrote, "no greater example than Greece of naked repression and nationalist jingoism in all Europe." The murder of 10,000 Polish officers in the Katyn forest, however, touched no such wellsprings of emotion. "If" the Russians were

[4] See especially Robert W. Tucker's *The Radical Left and American Foreign Policy* (Baltimore: The Johns Hopkins Press, 1971); Charles S. Maier, "Revisionism and the Interpretation of Cold War Origins," *Perspectives in American History* IV (1970), 313-347; and J. L. Richardson, "Cold War Revisionism: A Critique," *World Politics* XXIV (1972), 579-612. John Lewis Gaddis's *The United States and the Origins of the Cold War, 1941-1947* (New York: Columbia University Press, 1972), though an excellent interpretive work in its own right, offers a number of explicit and implicit criticisms of New Left revisionism. Both sides in the debate are represented in two recent anthologies: Thomas G. Paterson's *The Origins of the Cold War* (Lexington, Mass.: D. C. Heath, 1970); and James V. Compton's *America and the Origins of the Cold War* (Boston: Houghton Mifflin, 1972).

guilty, he concluded, "it must be suggested that Katyn was the exception rather than the rule."[5] The United States invariably wishes to "penetrate" Eastern Europe, in revisionist works, whereas the Soviet Union seeks merely "economic partnerships," a semantic distinction Eastern Europeans might grimly enjoy. The list can be extended indefinitely.

It has also been pointed out that New Left authors exaggerate the importance of evidence which supports their themes and minimize or ignore materials which do not. "One can not avoid concluding," J. L. Richardson has written, "that the revisionists violate the basic methodological rule formulated by Karl Popper, that one should seek to falsify rather than verify hypotheses."[6] This is particularly true regarding economic matters. Rightly complaining that orthodox historians often treated such issues as inconsequential, New Left scholars leave the impression that American policymakers thought of little else. Nowhere is this selectivity more obvious than in their use of the memoirs of men such as Harry S Truman, James F. Byrnes, and others. Notwithstanding that most of these accounts were published during the peak of the Cold War (when former officials were trying to show how anti-communist they had been all along), revisionists commonly quote the most grandiose and militant phrases from these volumes as though it were unnecessary even to ask whether they accurately reflected attitudes held years earlier. Contrary statements receive no

[5] Gabriel Kolko, *The Politics of War: The World and United States Foreign Policy, 1943-1945* (New York: Random House, 1968), 584, 106.

[6] Richardson, "Cold War Revisionism," 608.

such ready acceptance. In alleging that Lend-Lease curtailment in May 1945 represented an effort to coerce the Soviet Union, for instance, the revisionists omit or discount the fact that these same sources categorically deny any such intent.

Finally, there is the matter of Russian motives and goals, especially those of Stalin himself. Although the revisionists usually file disclaimers to the effect that they do not intend to present systematic analyses of Soviet foreign policy, they all too often proceed to judge Stalin's actions as though they were privy to his most confidential thoughts. Without hesitation they have pronounced as "frank" or "sincere" statements of his about which nothing more is known than that he made them, and they almost invariably construe his policies in the most favorable light.

The revisionists themselves argue that they have stood history right side up rather than on its head. Certainly orthodox historians have been guilty of precisely those charges now being levied against New Left scholars. Some have perceived within the Soviet system a dynamic of expansionism every bit as deterministic as the (hard) revisionists' version of American capitalism. They too have employed variations of the double-standard—the Americans and British "restore order" in an occupied area, the Russians "suppress dissident elements"—and often have written as though the Russians could have had no legitimate concerns about national security. Many *have* ignored economic relationships, as the revisionists claim, and have just as unhesitatingly attributed to Stalin objectives (malevolent, of course) for which no reliable evidence exists.

Thus far the debate has proceeded along lines similar to countless historiographical disputes over the years. The participants differ in which interpretations and hypotheses they think best explain an agreed-upon body of evidence. But *is* there agreement on the evidence? Most revisionist writing has been characterized by impressive —at times overwhelming—documentation from a wide variety of official and unofficial sources. These sources, they contend, directly support their theses. The instances are few where they have claimed that American policymakers were unconscious of their true motives, or that they deliberately misrepresented them in the written records. In the following chapters I have subjected to a very simple test seven of the most prominent New Left works offering interpretations of the Cold War's origins.[7] I have compared the evidence as presented by the revisionists with the sources from which the evidence was taken. The results are illuminating.

Granting a generous allowance for mere carelessness, such an analysis reveals that these books *without exception* are based upon pervasive misusages of the source materials. Although the frequency varies from volume to volume, even the best fails to attain the most flexible definition of scholarship. Stated briefly, the most striking characteristic of revisionist historiography has been the extent to which New Left authors have revised the

[7] This study is limited to those books purportedly based upon extensive research in primary source materials. The present writer wishes to emphasize that his focus is upon the methods used by the authors in question. Nothing herein should be construed as a defense either of some particular orthodox position or of American policy at the time.

evidence itself. And if the component parts of historical interpretations are demonstrably false, what can be said about the interpretations? They may yet be valid, but in the works examined they are often irrelevant to the data used to support them. Until this fact is recognized, there can be no realistic assessment of which elements of revisionism can justifiably be incorporated into new syntheses and which must be discarded altogether.

1.

THE TRAGEDY OF AMERICAN DIPLOMACY: WILLIAM APPLEMAN WILLIAMS

By far the most influential American revisionist interpreter of the origins of the Cold War has been William Appleman Williams. As early as 1952, a time when the political and intellectual climate was most uncongenial to such interpretations, Williams's *American-Russian Relations, 1781-1947* anticipated many of the themes later revisionists would amplify. Then, in 1959, his more sophisticated *The Tragedy of American Diplomacy* appeared, a book which a sympathetic scholar has called "perhaps the finest interpretive essay on American foreign policy ever written," and which even an unfriendly reviewer conceded was "brilliant."[1] In addition to his own writing, Williams inspired a number of younger scholars —some his own students—who themselves went on to publish variations on his themes. It is scarcely an exaggeration to say that much of the existing revisionist, or "New Left," literature on the subject amounts to little more than extended footnotes on interpretations Williams first put forward.

[1] (Cleveland: World, 1959; rev. and enl. edn., New York: Dell, 1962.) The first quotation is from David Horowitz's *The Free World Colossus* (rev. edn., New York: Hill and Wang, 1971), 4; the second from A. A. Berle, Jr.'s review of Williams's book in the *New York Times Book Review*, February 15, 1959.

13

In his earlier work, *American-Russian Relations,* Williams candidly admitted that the dearth of available documents limited him to presenting "no more than a review of the central features of recent relations between the United States and the Soviet Union."[2] Yet the basic framework upon which he would later elaborate was made clear. Contradicting the prevailing notion that the Cold War had come about through the actions of an aggressive and expansionist Soviet Union, Williams argued that the United States itself bore the primary responsibility. Even before Pearl Harbor, he wrote, American policymakers had committed themselves to achieving a postwar world dominated by an alliance between Great Britain and the United States. By attempting to force upon Russia this Anglo-American world order without regard to her minimum security needs, American leaders forced an essentially conservative Soviet Union into acting unilaterally in her own defense. Williams's analyses of the means through which the United States supposedly tried to coerce Russia—manipulation of Lend Lease and loans, brandishing atomic weapons, etc.—would later become staple items in revisionist fare.[3]

It was in *The Tragedy of American Diplomacy,* particularly the revised edition of 1962 (by which time important sources such as the *Potsdam Papers* had become available), that Williams spelled out his more mature views. The "tragedy" of American foreign policy, he contended, was the evolution of the Open Door Policy "from a utopian idea into an ideology, from an intellectual out-

[2] *American-Russian Relations, 1781-1947* (New York: Holt, Rinehart, 1952), 258.
[3] *Ibid.,* Chapter IX.

14

look for changing the world into one concerned with preserving it in the traditional mold."[4] Devised in the context of depression and the closing of the frontier in the 1890's, the Open Door Policy represented an effort to resolve the internal contradictions of capitalism—chronic overproduction, recurrent depression—without inducing fundamental change in the system itself. Applied originally as a means of securing equal access in China for American goods and investments but quickly extended to encompass the entire world, this policy came to be based upon "the firm conviction, even dogmatic belief, that America's *domestic* well-being depends upon such sustained, ever-increasing overseas economic expansion." The result, as Williams succinctly put it, was that "the history of the Open Door Notes became the history of American foreign relations from 1900 to 1958."[5]

Having enlarged the Open Door concept into a global policy, he continued, American policymakers defined any effort by other powers to obstruct this goal as threatening to the existence of the American system, predicated as it was on the need for unhindered expansion. Of all the twentieth-century American presidents, only Franklin D. Roosevelt recognized the dangers inherent in such an approach. At times F.D.R. appeared to be moving tentatively toward restructuring the American society as a way out of the dilemma, but during his last months "he was turning back toward the inadequate domestic programs of the New Deal era, and was in foreign affairs reasserting the traditional strategy of the Open Door Policy." His successor, Harry S Truman, who failed even to apprehend the problem, seemed "to react, think, and act as an almost

[4] *Tragedy*, 205-206.   [5] *Ibid.*, 11, 45.

classic personification of the entire Open Door Policy."[6] He and his advisors pursued ends that made the Cold War inevitable.

In contrast with the United States' global pretensions, according to Williams, Russian objectives were far more limited. Stalin resolved the contradiction between "the expansive prophecy of Marx about world revolution" and "a realistic, Marxian analysis of world conditions" in a most conservative manner.[7] He was adamant on only three points: Russia must obtain friendly governments on her western periphery, the wherewithal to rebuild her war-torn economy, and guarantees that Germany would not again become a threat to her safety. Everything else was negotiable. Had the United States helped—or merely permitted—Russia to gain these modest ends, there would have been no Cold War. But in their quest for an Open Door in Eastern Europe (which to Williams meant the existence of pro-Western governments there), American leaders contested the first of Russia's minimum conditions and subsequently pursued strategies which jeopardized the other two.

The mortal weakness of Williams's interpretation lay in his inability to produce even the scantiest evidence that American policymakers actually regarded an Open Door in Eastern Europe as the critical factor, rather than as one of many subsidiary goals, in relations with Russia. In lieu of such evidence he quoted a number of government officials and businessmen on the overall importance of trade and investment in the postwar world.[8] None of the statements cited were made with any particular ref-

6 *Ibid.*, 205, 239.   7 *Ibid.*, 206.
8 *Ibid.*, 232-239.

16

erence to Eastern Europe, however, nor did Williams even try (except through his own repeated assertions) to demonstrate that the authors of those comments considered Eastern Europe as a very important factor in their assessments. Using the same procedures he could have as convincingly shown that American leaders were desperately concerned with achieving an Open Door in even the most insignificant areas.

In the single passage where he did put forward material having to do specifically with Eastern Europe, Williams wrote as follows:

> By the end of the month, in preparation for the Potsdam Conference, the American position concerning the countries of eastern Europe had become clear and firm. The United States planned "to insist on the reorganization of the present governments or the holding of free general elections." The broad objective was phrased in the classic terms of the Open Door Policy: "To permit American nationals to enter, move about freely and carry on commercial and government operations unmolested in the countries in question."
>
> The goal was "access, on equal terms, to such trade, raw materials and industry" as existed and developed. In the meantime, such access was sought "to modify existing arrangements." As part of that general effort, American officials planned to demand unrestricted movement for American newspapermen so that "the spotlight [can be] trained on these areas."[9]

In reality, this "clear and firm" policy Williams constructed himself by mixing together portions of three separate position papers, only one of which had anything at all

[9] *Ibid.*, 245.

to do with economic matters. That document, the primary topic of which was the removal by Russian forces of some American-owned oil equipment, did recommend that the President request from Stalin agreements which would amount to an Open Door in Eastern Europe.[10] But it contained nothing to suggest that the United States "planned 'to insist on the reorganization of the present governments or the holding of free general elections' " in pursuit of such arrangements. The phrase, taken from another paper, applied only to Bulgaria and Rumania. Its author advocated such a course towards those two nations "to attain at least the same position for which we have consistently striven" in Czechoslovakia, Yugoslavia, and Poland (whose governments the United States already had recognized), "where there are some elements not completely subservient to Moscow. . . ." The failure to take this stand, he warned, might encourage the Soviet Union to repeat its actions "in countries farther to the west."[11] The quotation having to do with newspapermen likewise appeared in a document which made no mention of economic issues.[12] In short, the "American position" advanced by Williams consisted of far more than the sum of its actual parts.

How could a policy of such transcendent importance have left so few traces in the records as to have compelled Williams to resort to such procedures? One might reason-

---

[10] *Foreign Relations of the United States, Diplomatic Papers: The Conference of Berlin (The Potsdam Conference), 1945* (2 vols., Washington, D.C.: Government Printing Office, 1960), I, 420-423. Hereafter cited as *Potsdam Papers*.

[11] *Ibid.*, 357-362   [12] *Ibid.*, 318-320.

ably expect the sources to be brimming with references to the drive to obtain an Open Door in Eastern Europe. Not so, Williams argued in an earlier passage. "American leaders had internalized, and had come to *believe*, the theory, the necessity, and the morality of open-door expansion," he wrote. "Hence they seldom thought it necessary to explain or defend the approach."[13]

Whatever the validity of this "proof by lack of evidence" thesis, Williams himself contradicted it in his own pages. Referring to American goals in Manchuria, he showed through copious quotations that American officials, most notably Secretary of War Henry L. Stimson and W. Averell Harriman, Ambassador to Russia, were very much concerned to maintain the Open Door in that area. "Stimson," Williams wrote, "seems to have set himself the role of special tutor to Truman and [Secretary of State] Byrnes on the importance of the Open Door Policy in the Far East."[14] Why American policymakers had no need to mention the Open Door in Eastern Europe because the policy had become "internalized," yet referred to it frequently and by name in discussions over Manchuria (the site of its original application), Williams failed to make clear. Equally mysterious is why Stimson should feel the need to appoint himself "special tutor" to a man whom Williams described as the "classic personification" of the Open Door Policy. It is difficult to escape the conclusion that where Williams had the facts he used them, and where he could find none he claimed their very absence corroborated his interpretation.

[13] *Tragedy*, 206 (Williams's emphasis).
[14] *Ibid.*, 245-246

Williams devoted a good deal of attention to the Potsdam Conference (July 16–August 2, 1945), using it to show how American officials pursued their strategies. Stalin, according to Williams, came to Potsdam in quest of humble goals: "He was still concerned about Russia's frontiers in Europe, about preventing Germany from trying it all over in another 25 years, and about a major economic transfusion for the Soviet Union's battered economy."[15] Convinced that the United States possessed effective economic leverage, emboldened by reports of the successful atomic tests (which arrived as the conference got under way), American negotiators sought to force Russian acquiescence in Eastern Europe by denying her even these minimum demands. Williams's version of the discussions at Potsdam supported his theme, but scarcely resembles what actually took place.

One of the techniques Williams used most often in *Tragedy* was to construct imaginary speeches and dialogues by splicing together phrases uttered at different times and on diverse subjects. His presentation of Stalin's opening statements at the first plenary meeting is typical:

> "This council," Stalin remarked in explaining the Soviet view of the conference at its first general session, "will deal with reparations and will give an indication of the day when the Peace Conference should meet." The primary political issue, he continued, was that of dealing with Germany and its former allies. That was "high policy. The purpose of such a policy was to separate these countries from Germany as a great force." Recurring often to the "many difficulties and sacrifices"

[15] *Ibid.*, 246.

brought upon Russia by those Axis partners, Stalin argued that the proper strategy was "to detach them once and for all from Germany." As for reparations, Russia would if necessary "compel" such deliveries.[16]

Stalin made no such speech. His reference on the opening day to "This council" did not even refer to the Potsdam Conference itself; in context the Russian was making a clarifying statement about Truman's proposal that a *Council* of Foreign Ministers be formed.[17] The other phrases Williams quoted were taken from various parts of a discussion held three days later on another American proposal, this one concerning the treatment of Germany's former allies. Stalin approved the proposal in substance, suggesting only minor changes. And his comment about compelling reparations deliveries did not apply to reparations *for* Russia, as Williams has it, but to Bulgarian reparations for Greece and Yugoslavia, which is quite a different matter.[18]

Williams's account of the way American negotiators reacted to Stalin's alleged emphasis upon reparations is equally misleading. " 'Reparations,' " Williams quoted Byrnes as telling Molotov on July 20, " 'do not seem to the United States to be an immediate problem.' " This response, in *Tragedy*, is presented as "crucial to the outcome of the Potsdam Conference, and also, very probably, to the whole course of subsequent events."[19] Byrnes, according to Williams, was trying to capitalize on Russia's reconstruction needs by refusing to offer post-war loans on the one hand, and by obstructing equitable rep-

[16] *Ibid.*, 246-247.
[18] *Ibid.*, 172-173.
[17] *Potsdam Papers* II, 62.
[19] *Tragedy*, 247.

21

arations settlements on the other. The Americans believed they could "bargain from a position of formidable power," in Williams's view, because *"Byrnes knew, when he told Molotov on July 20 that reparations were not 'an immediate problem,' that the atom bomb was a success."*[20] But what Williams neglected to mention was that Byrnes's statement did not pertain to reparations from Germany, which was the crux of the matter; he was telling Molotov that since the United States at the time was pouring money into Italy to keep her from going under, reparations *from Italy* were not "an immediate problem."[21] Byrnes's remark, when read in its proper context, is irrelevant to Williams's thesis.

The United States altered its position on reparations (though not its ultimate goals) a few days later, one learns in *Tragedy*, when it became clear that Russia would not back off from her demands regardless of American economic power or possession of the bomb. On July 23, therefore, Byrnes proposed that each nation take reparations from its own zone of occupation. This suggestion, to Williams, meant "that the Russians would have a free hand in their zone of Germany and throughout eastern Europe" because "the freedom to control economics implied—demanded—political control." Yet, *"the fascinating thing is that the Russians fought that proposal for one whole week—from July 23 to July 31—before Stalin finally*

[20] *Ibid.*, 248 (Williams's emphasis).
[21] *Potsdam Papers* II, 148. The entire statement reads: "Mr. Byrnes pointed out that the United States Government has already advanced $200,000,000 to Italy and would probably have to advance $400,000,000 or $500,000,000 more. Therefore reparations do not seem to the United States to be an immediate problem."

agreed to it. Even then, he remarked very sharply that it was 'the opposite of liberal.' "[22]

Why did the Russians oppose such an offer, and why did the United States make it? The answer to both questions, according to Williams, is that the American proposal would have denied Russia badly needed industrial equipment from the Ruhr Valley (which lay within the Western zone) and excluded her from participating in the control of German industry. By refusing to tie the question of German war potential to that of reparations, Williams wrote, the United States could afford to make concessions on the latter issue because it still possessed as tools the bomb and Russian fear of a resurgent Germany. "American leaders were certain that the bomb, and Russia's great recovery needs," as he put it, "provided them with the leverage to re-establish the Open Door, and pro-Western governments, in eastern Europe."[23]

The evidence Williams cited to prove this "new" strategy is as spurious as that he used to substantiate the old one. In order to show that American officials understood that the "meaning" of the arrangement that each power would take reparations from its own zone was that it would in effect "give Russia a free hand," Williams cited a "memorandum" written by Assistant Secretary of State Will Clayton after the Conference adjourned:

> Although he was formally denying the point he was raising, the tone of his remarks needs no comment. "There appears to be," he noted ruefully, "an unfortunate tendency to interpret the reparations operating agreement as an indication of complete abandonment

[22] *Tragedy*, 250 (Williams's emphasis).
[23] *Ibid.*, 253.

23

of four power treatment of Germany. This is not stated in the texts and should not be accepted as a necessary conclusion. . . ."[24]

Thus, Clayton is made to seem as though he were complaining about how the participants at the Conference interpreted the agreement. That is incorrect. The Assistant Secretary's words were taken from a cable (not a "memorandum") he directed to subordinate officials back in Washington who he believed had gotten the wrong impression about what had been done. The rest of his message, omitted in *Tragedy*, consisted of a detailed effort to show how the arrangements would be worked out within the framework of "common policies."[25]

As further evidence for his interpretation, Williams described how Molotov "raised—very directly and without any frills—the central implication of the proposal that Byrnes had offered on July 23."

> MR. MOLOTOV: My understanding, Secretary Byrnes, is that you have in mind the proposal that each country should take reparations from its own zone. If we fail to reach an agreement the result will be the same. . . .
>
> THE SECRETARY [Byrnes]: Yes. . . .
>
> MR. MOLOTOV: said would not the Secretary's suggestion mean that each country would have a free hand in their own zone and would act entirely independently of the others?
>
> THE SECRETARY [Byrnes]: said that was true in substance. . . .[26]

[24] *Ibid.*, 250.   [25] *Potsdam Papers* II, 938-940.
[26] *Tragedy*, 251.

This "exchange" also misrepresented what the documents contain. First, Molotov's remarks were not made in a single conversation, as Williams presented them; they were taken from notes on two separate meetings. Far more important, Williams's use of ellipses distorted the sense of Byrnes's replies. In response to Molotov's query about each country's having a "free hand," for instance, Byrnes said "that was true in substance but he had in mind working out arrangements for the exchange of needed products between the zones, for example, from the Ruhr if the British agreed, machinery and equipment could be removed and exchanged with the Soviet authorities for goods—food and coal—in the Soviet zone." Williams also failed to mention that Byrnes assured Molotov "that under his scheme nothing was changed in regard to overall treatment of German finance, transport, foreign trade, etc."[27] By culling out phrases and isolated sentences from the sources, Williams badly garbled what Byrnes's proposal was all about and how the Russians reacted to it.

As a final example of his contention that both the Americans and Russians understood that Byrnes's proposal meant giving over political control to each nation in its own zone, Williams alluded to a conversation among the heads-of-state during which, he said, Stalin "extended" Byrnes's proposal "in a way that clearly foreshadowed the division of Europe. The specific issue involved the assignment of German assets in other European countries, but the discussion immediately picked up overtones of a far broader nature."

[27] *Potsdam Papers* II, 439-440, 450, 474.

PREMIER STALIN: . . . with regard to shares and foreign investments, perhaps the demarcation lines between the Soviet and Western zones of occupation should be taken as the dividing lines and everything west of that line would go to the Allies and everything east of that line to the Russians.

THE PRESIDENT [TRUMAN] inquired if he meant a line running from the Baltic to the Adriatic.

PREMIER STALIN replied in the affirmative. . . .

[BRITISH FOREIGN SECRETARY] BEVIN said he agreed and asked if Greece would belong to Britain. . . .

PREMIER STALIN suggested that the Allies take Yugoslavia and Austria would be divided into zones. . . .

MR. BYRNES said he thought it was important to have a meeting of minds. Mr. Bevin's question was whether the Russians' claim was limited to the zone occupied by the Russian Army. To that he understood Mr. Stalin to say "yes." If that were so he was prepared to agree.

PREMIER STALIN replied in the affirmative. . . .

THE PRESIDENT [TRUMAN] said that he agreed with the Soviet proposal.[28]

Once again, Williams's use of hiatuses abused the historical record. A look at the entire exchange reveals that the discussions never deviated from the subject of German investments and assets, nor did they at any time "pick up overtones of a far broader nature."[29] Williams himself produced this effect by selecting appropriate comments scattered throughout the talks and placing

[28] *Tragedy*, 252.
[29] *Potsdam Papers* II, 566-569.

them sequentially as though they constituted a sustained conversation.

He employed similar methods to make it appear that Stalin looked upon Byrnes's plan as "the opposite of liberal" because of his fear of a resurgent Germany. In his passages on this question, Williams claimed that the Russians tried to discuss as related matters reparations and Germany's demilitarization, but that the United States refused to do so:

> Molotov connected the issues of reparations and German war potential very simply: "The question of reparations was even more urgent because unless this was settled there could be no progress on economic matters" involving the future strength of German industry. Hence the Soviets wanted "clear replies to the questions."

"Finally," according to Williams, "in the face of continued American refusal to discuss the issues in that related way, Stalin accepted the Byrnes proposal of July 23, 1945."[30]

It should be pointed out in the first place that Stalin never called Byrnes's plan "the opposite of liberal." Williams transplanted a phrase the Russian leader had uttered during a discussion over two percentage figures on the exchange of goods between zones. Stalin's figures were accepted.[31] Molotov's statement beginning "The question of reparations. . . ," moreover, constituted his entire comment on the matter of priorities in setting up an agenda, a request to which Byrnes agreed.[32] Williams converted the remark into an expression of alarm over the implications of the American plan by adding the

[30] *Tragedy*, 251-252.   [31] *Potsdam Papers* II, 516-517.
[32] *Ibid.*, 425.

phrase "involving the future strength of German industry." The statement about the Soviets wanting "clear replies to the questions," taken from a different page in the source, in context referred to a report submitted by the Reparations Commission (upon which a Russian member sat).[33] Placing these elements together as though they represented an exchange over the question of Germany's war potential showed remarkable ingenuity but rather small concern for fealty to the sources.

Throughout his account of the negotiations at Potsdam, Williams repeatedly asserted that American officials acted as they did out of their determination to achieve an Open Door in Eastern Europe. He did not, however, produce any evidence that this was true. In the source he used for his analysis, the *Potsdam Papers*, the sole reference to an Open Door made at the Conference appeared as the last sentence in an American proposal headed USE OF ALLIED PROPERTY FOR SATELLITE REPARATIONS OR "WAR TROPHIES." This proposal was circulated on July 25, accepted by the Conference "on principle," and the drafting of an agreement on the matter was left to be worked out through normal diplomatic channels.[34] The

[33] *Ibid.*, 428. "MR. MOLOTOV said that the Soviet delegation regarded the work done by the Commission on Reparations as unsatisfactory. He said that they should have *clear replies to the questions* under discussion or should direct them to other channels in case they were unable to solve them themselves." (Emphasis added.)

[34] *Potsdam Papers* II, 545-546, 744-745, 1498.

Since the completion of this manuscript a new revisionist work has appeared, Bruce Kuklick's *American Policy and the Division of Germany: The Clash with Russia over Reparations* (Ithaca: Cornell University Press, 1972). Like Williams, Kuklick argues that the United States at Potsdam departed from the Yalta agree-

issue of an Open Door was discussed neither at the heads-of-state level nor in the conferences of the foreign ministers.

Perhaps, as Williams claimed, American officials had so "internalized" the Open Door Policy that they felt no need to discuss it among themselves. It is very odd, however, that they failed to call Stalin's attention to it. How could they expect the various strategies Williams assigned to them to work if Stalin himself did not know what it

---

ments on reparations as a means of forcing Russia to grant the American demand for "multilateralism" (a variation of Williams's Open Door) in Eastern Europe. Although somewhat more accurate in his handling of sources than most revisionists, Kuklick has written a grievously flawed book. In contending that Roosevelt at Yalta committed the United States to a reparations figure of approximately 20 billion dollars (half to go to Russia) when he consented to use this amount as the "basis" for future discussions, for instance, Kuklick unaccountably fails to mention the "considerations" upon which this sum was based. Among these were estimates of Germany's national wealth, the amount of destruction likely to be caused by the war, and what would be necessary to provide Germany with "living standards comparable to those prevailing in Central Europe." Presumably the actual reparations figure would be adjusted on the basis of how widely the situation at war's end differed from Russian estimates. By the time of the Postdam Conference, however, these estimates were irrelevant. The Soviet Union had turned over to Poland almost one-fifth of prewar Germany, the remaining four-fifths would have to sustain the population (8½ million) of the ceded area, Russia had stripped away whatever she could under the name of "war booty" (not to be counted as reparations), and no systematic evaluation of actual war damage had been carried out. Thus, as one American official put it, the "situation was radically altered" by the time of the Potsdam Conference. Kuklick mentions some of these facts but, despite overwhelming evidence to the contrary (see *Potsdam Papers* II, 830ff.), asserts that they did not figure importantly in American thinking. He also converts

was they were trying to achieve? Coercion rarely succeeds when the victim is kept unaware of what he is expected to concede in order to get relief. Under close scrutiny, Williams's thesis translates into a series of imaginary tactics designed to achieve unstated goals. This cannot be taken seriously as historical analysis.

Williams's handling of the Potsdam Conference exemplifies the standard of scholarship found throughout the pages of *Tragedy*. Referring to the conference at Yalta (February 4-11, 1945), for instance, he has Stalin going

---

the quotation referring to a "radically altered" *situation* into one supporting the notion that the United States "radically altered" *Allied diplomacy* toward Germany (147). The correct version contradicts Kuklick's thesis that the United States refused to accept the Yalta figure for ulterior purposes; his own version supports it.

His handling of specific issues aside, Kuklick's work dramatically exposes a weakness which has become more obvious as each new revisionist book appears—a total lack of direct evidence. Given the scarcity of sources ten or fifteen years ago, it was plausible to construct on the basis of circumstantial evidence the "real" American policy on reparations as opposed to the official version. But an enormous body of documentary materials has since become available, materials consisting of what American policymakers were saying and writing to one another at the time. Had Kuklick handled the sources he used with perfect fidelity, his thesis still would rest upon the following propositions: (a) that in the countless memoranda, instructions, cables, etc., now accessible, no one at any time so much as hinted at a "strategy" of enormous significance; (b) that the stated objectives in these documents are fictitious (to mislead whom? other officials?) or else were written in a kind of code everyone understood; and (c) that American policymakers somehow neglected to convey to Stalin the terms of the "deal"—multilateralism as the price for loans or reparations—they were trying to force upon him. Acceptance of these propositions calls for an act of faith not usually associated with historical inquiry.

there "with two approaches to the postwar world. One was based on receiving a large loan from the United States. His overtures in this direction were answered with vague and unrewarding replies."[35] Actually, Stalin made no mention of this matter at Yalta. The only reference to it occurred during the following exchange:

> MR. MOLOTOV indicated that the Soviet Government expected to receive reparations from Germany in kind and hoped that the United States would furnish the Soviet Union with long-term credits.
>
> [Secretary of State] MR. STETTINIUS stated that his Government had studied this question and that he personally was ready to discuss it at any time with Mr. Molotov. This could be done here as well as later either in Moscow or in Washington.[36]

The subject was not raised again through the entire conference. Stalin's "overtures" and the United States' "vague and unrewarding replies" existed only in Williams's imagination.

Again on the subject of a loan, which bulks large in *Tragedy*, Williams contended that Secretary Byrnes "had neither time nor interest for the idea of working out some agreement with the Russians. . . ." Byrnes, according to Williams, "even sidetracked the basic memorandum dealing with the issue. 'I had it placed in the "Forgotten File," ' he later revealed, 'as I felt sure that Fred Vinson, the new Secretary of the Treasury, would not press it.' "[37]

[35] *Tragedy*, 223.

[36] *Foreign Relations of the United States, Diplomatic Papers: The Conferences at Malta and Yalta, 1945* (Washington, D.C.: Government Printing Office, 1955), 610. Hereafter cited as *Yalta Papers*.

[37] *Tragedy*, 239.

But the "it" Byrnes placed in the "Forgotten File" was not, as Williams claimed, the "basic memorandum" on the issue. It was a memorandum written by the former Secretary of the Treasury, Henry Morgenthau, Jr., which suggested a *larger* loan at a *lower* interest rate than the Russians themselves had asked for.[38] Whatever Byrnes's culpability in the failure of negotiations for a loan, the evidence Williams cited was irrelevant to the issue.

Concerning the atomic bomb, Williams stated unequivocally that "the United States dropped the bomb to end the war against Japan *and thereby stop the Russians in Asia, and to give them sober pause in eastern Europe.*" Part of his evidence for this interpretation is contained in the following paragraph:

> The decision to bomb Japan as quickly as possible was made during the Potsdam Conference, and at the very time of the toughest discussions about eastern Europe. In a very candid meeting on July 23, 1945, Truman, General George C. Marshall, Stimson and others generally agreed that the Russians were no longer needed in the war against Japan. They also talked very directly of using the bomb before the Russians could enter that conflict. Actually, however, that was not a new approach. Stimson had recommended as early as July 2, 1945, that the bomb should be dropped at a time when "the Russian attack, if actual, must not have progressed too far." And once it had proved out in the test, Truman was "intensely pleased" with the chance of using it before the Russians even entered the war.[39]

[38] James F. Byrnes, *All in One Lifetime* (New York: Harper and Brothers, 1958), 310.

[39] *Tragedy*, 253-254 (Williams's emphasis).

There was no such meeting on July 23. At Truman's request Stimson did ask Marshall that day whether "we needed the Russians in the war or whether we could get along without them." But the question was not asked in the context of "using the bomb before the Russians could enter that conflict"; it was asked because the Russians had refused thus far to be pinned down to specifying a date when they would join in. Each time the subject was raised, Stalin or Molotov replied that negotiations with China had to be concluded to Russian satisfaction before they would move against Japan. Marshall's reply is of interest, too. He said the United States could manage alone, but not for the reason Williams indicated. The United States had desired Russian participation, Marshall said, in order to engage the Japanese Manchurian army and prevent it from returning to the home islands. The mere presence of Russian forces along the Manchurian border was accomplishing that purpose. "But he pointed out that even if we went ahead in the war without the Russians," according to Stimson's diary, "and compelled the Japanese to surrender to our terms, that would not prevent the Russians from marching into Manchuria anyhow and striking, thus permitting them to get virtually what they wanted in the surrender terms."[40] So much for Williams's assertion that the Americans thought they could "stop the Russians in Asia" by dropping the bomb.

The rest of Williams's paragraph is similarly erroneous. Stimson's recommendation of July 2, written before the atomic test was carried out, contained no mention of

[40] Excerpt from Stimson's diary, *Potsdam Papers* II, 1324.

33

that potential weapon. His suggestion was that a sincere effort be made to secure Japan's surrender before an invasion began. He proposed that, at the proper time, a solemn warning be conveyed to Japan "by the chief representatives of the United States, Great Britain, China and, if then a belligerent, Russia, calling upon Japan to surrender. . . ." His point was that this had to be done before the final struggle began, for the Japanese "when actually locked with the enemy will fight to the very death." Therefore, Stimson noted, "the Russian attack, if actual, must not have progressed too far" by the time the warning was issued.[41] Williams took similar liberties with Truman's words. The President was "intensely pleased," according to the source, solely by reports that the atomic program was proceeding ahead of schedule. Nothing in the document suggests that the "chance of using it [the bomb] before the Russians even entered the war" figured in his emotional state.[42]

Williams's cavalier treatment of his sources resulted in a number of enduring revisionist myths, none more popular than what might be called "The Wallace Letter Episode." In trying to show how rigidly America's Cold War posture had set in by the Spring of 1946, Williams produced the following paragraph:

> American representatives persistently tied such aid [a loan] to the question of the Open Door Policy in eastern Europe. Secretary of Commerce [Henry A.] Wallace warned Truman on March 14, 1946, that such an ap-

[41] Stimson's memorandum is reprinted in his and McGeorge Bundy's *On Active Service in Peace and War* (New York: Harper and Brothers, 1948), 620-624.
[42] *Potsdam Papers* II, 1373.

proach was increasing the tension. He suggested that it would be more fruitful "to talk with them in an understanding way" about "their dire economic needs and of their disturbed sense of security." Contrary to the impression created by all the vicious attacks on Wallace, he was not proposing anything that could be called appeasement. He wanted a calm and less adamant approach to economic discussions as a means of persuading the Russians to modify "many of their assumptions and conclusions which stand in the way of peaceful world cooperation." Wallace wanted neither to demand or to surrender but only to bargain in a mature fashion. But quite in keeping with his support for Churchill, Truman reports that he "ignored this letter of Wallace's." Note that the President does not say merely that he considered but finally rejected Wallace's analysis and proposal. He "ignored" it. In that difference lies considerable insight into the state of the cold war as of March 1946.[43]

All this is solemn nonsense. Whatever the validity of Williams's assertion about tying loans to the Open Door —he offered no evidence that this was so—Wallace's letter had nothing to do with the issue. On the contrary, Wallace specifically stated that he was *not* writing about "negotiations related to immediate proposals such as a loan." Nor did he criticize any particular American action, as the sentences from which Williams quoted make clear when read in full:

> We know that much of the recent Soviet behavior which has caused us concern has been the result of *their dire economic needs and of their disturbed sense of security.* . . . To do this [convince them of "our sincere

[43] *Tragedy*, 260-261.

devotion to the cause of peace"], it is necessary *to talk with them in an understanding way*, with full realization of their difficulties and yet with emphasis on the lack of realism in *many of their assumptions and conclusions which stand in the way of peaceful world cooperation.*[44]

By rearranging these phrases, Williams made it appear that Wallace was urging Truman to *reverse* American policy when in reality the Secretary was proposing that an effort be made to *explain* the policies so as to correct "the lack of realism in many of their assumptions and conclusions."

By citing only the phrases he did, Williams created the impression that Truman's comment that he "ignored this letter of Wallace's" applied to the latter's desire for more amicable relations with Russia. Actually, the substance of Wallace's letter lay in his proposal that a special team of economic experts (which he modestly offered to name) be empowered to negotiate on long-range issues with Russia outside regular diplomatic channels. Truman, citing the fact that he had just named a new ambassador to the Soviet Union earlier that month, reproduced the letter in his *Memoirs* to substantiate his claim that Wallace meddled in affairs beyond his jurisdiction.[45] It was the Wallace proposal Truman said he ignored, not the Secretary's plea for better relations with Russia.

Williams's use of evidence throughout *Tragedy* bears a marked resemblance to those "composite photographs" favored by the more sensational tabloids earlier in the

[44] Wallace's letter is reprinted in Harry S Truman's *Memoirs, Volume I: Year of Decisions* (New York: Doubleday, 1955), 555-556 (emphasis added).

[45] *Ibid.*

century. By superimposing the faces of prominent individuals upon the bodies of posed models (usually in compromising positions), editors were able to obtain pictures of anything their vivid imaginations required. Williams achieved the same effect through his handling of quotations. By weaving into his own prose phrases and sentences gathered from various contexts, he was able to create the appearance of authenticity for his theses where none existed. The result indeed was a "brilliant" piece of work, but one largely divorced from reality. The "tragedy" is that his book has been taken so seriously by those who ought to have known better.

2.

THE COLD WAR AND ITS ORIGINS: D. F. FLEMING

PINNING labels on historians is a hazardous enterprise at best, but in general the terms "New Left" and "revisionist" are synonymous when applied to interpretations of how the Cold War began. D. F. Fleming is an exception. He wrote his massive, two-volume *The Cold War and Its Origins* as an unreconstructed Wilsonian, not as a critic of the American system as such.[1] To Fleming, the train of events in 1945 which led to the Cold War closely paralleled what happened at the close of World War I. In the first instance, vindictive, backward-looking "isolationists" had sabotaged the structure of international collective security Woodrow Wilson had worked to create. In the second, vehement "anti-communists" undermined Franklin Delano Roosevelt's attempt to achieve a stable postwar world based upon cooperation between Great Britain and the United States on the one hand, and Russia on the other. In both cases Fleming blamed individuals rather than the imperatives of capitalism. A critique of his work is included here because he usually (if indiscriminately) is lumped together with the New Left and, more importantly, because a number of his interpretations of specific issues have become standard in New Left historiography.

[1] (New York: Doubleday, 1961.) All references in this essay are to Volume I, covering the period 1917-1950.

39

Fleming's thesis, in its broad outlines, is straightforward and unsubtle. Roosevelt and his Secretary of State Cordell Hull had worked throughout the war to build a sound relationship with the Soviet Union. They had succeeded, despite various disagreements which inevitably crop up during times of stress, and both were optimistic that cooperation between the two powers could continue beyond the end of the war. Then, when ill-health removed Hull from the scene and Roosevelt died in April 1945, the carefully nurtured partnership began to collapse. Harry S Truman, "overwhelmed by the tremendous responsibilities suddenly placed upon him" and greatly influenced by men who wished to reverse F.D.R.'s policies, embarked upon a course that made the Cold War inevitable.[2] Stalin tried to preserve the coalition, and room for accommodation still existed as late as the Potsdam Conference in the Summer of 1945. Having acquired the atomic bomb by that time, however, the United States proceeded to launch a post-Hiroshima "diplomatic offensive," the goals of which violated Russia's minimal security needs in Eastern Europe. The failure of this offensive caused Truman by the Fall of 1945 to formulate in his own mind the basic elements of the "Truman Doctrine," which institutionalized the conflict.

The Cold War and Its Origins is detailed and wide in scope, with excursions into Congressional, journalistic, and public opinion, sometimes including even the author's own attitudes at the moment certain events took place. Its format verges on chaos, with chapters divided into seemingly innumerable subdivisions usually headed by rhetorical questions such as "How Could Poland Have

[2] *Cold War*, 266.

40

Been Saved for the West?" or "Should the A-bomb Secrets be Kept?" Then, too, its author failed to establish a sustained view of American motives. Without attempting to reconcile the contradictions, he attributed to American leaders simultaneously the most calculated violations of Russo-American collaboration and genuine efforts to reach accord. For all these reasons a systematic analysis of the volume is impossible in the space of an essay. Instead, a few of his interpretations which have become most popular in New Left circles will be examined in depth and used as points of departure for observations on his overall approach.

One of his basic themes is that Truman destroyed a fundamentally sound relationship between the United States and the Soviet Union. Fleming's assessment of that relationship at the time of Roosevelt's death emphasized those sources—some of dubious relevance—that corroborated his thesis and minimized or ignored those that did not. Two examples will illustrate his use of evidence. He quoted extensively from Edgar Snow's account of an interview with Roosevelt before the latter's death. Snow reported that F.D.R. had been extremely optimistic during their talk, and among other things recalled the President as having said "*I am convinced that we are going to get along* [with the Russians]." Fleming set great store by Snow's report and pronounced as "well based" his judgement that ensuing developments would not have caused Roosevelt to act as Truman did.[3] Leaving aside the question of whether Roosevelt would have informed a reporter of any misgivings he might have held, the point is that the Snow interview took place on March 3, only

[3] *Ibid.*, 215 (Fleming's emphasis).

41

three weeks after the Yalta Conference. Most sources agree that F.D.R. was confident at this stage, but the series of disagreements over carrying out the Yalta accords, which Truman inherited, had just then begun to arise.

The contrast between Fleming's reliance on Snow's speculation about how Roosevelt would have acted and his handling of harder evidence pointing to the opposite conclusion is illuminating. On April 1, less than two weeks before his death, Roosevelt and British Prime Minister Winston S. Churchill sent personal messages to Stalin protesting Russia's interpretation of the Yalta accords as they provided for the creation of a provisional government for Poland. Commenting on Russia's demand that the existing Soviet-sponsored Lublin Government should have the right to decide which other Poles should be called in for consultation, F.D.R. informed Stalin that " 'any such solution which would result in a thinly disguised continuance of the present government would be entirely unacceptable, and would cause our people to regard the Yalta agreement as a failure.' "[4] Fleming devoted but a single sentence to this message, did not quote from it, and described it merely as an expression of "concern with the development of events since Yalta."[5] He failed even to mention Roosevelt's cable to Churchill on the same subject, parts of which are reprinted on the very page of the source he cited for the April 1 communiqué. Roosevelt confided to Churchill his grave apprehensions, saying he was " 'acutely aware of the dangers inherent in

[4] Quoted in James F. Byrnes, *Speaking Frankly* (New York: Harper & Brothers, 1947), 54.

[5] *Cold War*, 211.

the present course of events, not only for the immediate issue involved but also for the San Francisco Conference [founding conference of the United Nations] and future world co-operation.' "[6] Since Stalin refused to modify his stand in his reply to F.D.R., the latter's statements would appear to provide a far more reliable guide to his attitude at the time of his death than his talk with Snow a month earlier.

Fleming's handling of Truman's first weeks in office is equally questionable. In a section of his book headed "Sudden Reversal," Fleming attributed Truman's alleged abandonment of Rooseveltian diplomacy to the influence of Fleet Admiral William D. Leahy, Chief of Staff to the President. As Leahy briefed the new President daily, and as the Admiral "had a long-time aversion to the Russians," Fleming without further evidence assigned to him the primary responsibility for Truman's "sudden reversal" of F.D.R.'s policies. Indeed, according to Fleming, "Leahy worked so rapidly that a week after his first conference the new President was ready to reprimand the Russians strongly."[7] His source for this revelation? A breezy, anecdotal article on Leahy published in *Colliers* magazine in 1948, a piece from which Fleming quoted no less than six times on one page.[8]

As for Truman's "reprimand" of Molotov, Fleming's version of the events surrounding their meeting established a model for a number of revisionist works. By minimizing or ignoring Russian moves during the period immediately preceding their confrontation, by selectively

[6] Quoted in Byrnes, *Speaking Frankly*, 54.

[7] *Cold War*, 266.

[8] Frank Gervasi, "Watchdog in the White House," *Colliers* 122 (October 9, 1948).

quoting only the more colorful phrases spoken, and by using highly emotive language to describe Truman's behavior, he exaggerated the new President's militance just as earlier he had exaggerated F.D.R.'s optimism.

Fleming began with an account of a meeting Truman called with his advisors on April 23, shortly before receiving Molotov. Secretary of State Edward R. Stettinius opened the session by announcing that discussions with the Russian Minister had bogged down over the status of the Lublin Government, particularly with reference to inviting it to send representatives to the San Francisco Conference. That government, Stettinius asserted, did not represent the Polish people. Truman then asked each of the participants to express his view on how the United States should proceed. Although Secretary of War Stimson, Admiral Leahy, and Army Chief of Staff George C. Marshall urged caution, Fleming wrote, Secretary of the Navy James G. Forrestal and others were for " 'a showdown with them now rather than later.' " Truman "came down heavily" on the latter side and stated

> "that he felt our agreements with the Soviet Union so far had been a one-way street and that he could not continue; it was now or never. He intended to go on with the plans for San Francisco and if the Russians did not wish to join us they could go to hell."

"This decision," to Fleming, "brings out strikingly the great rapidity with which Roosevelt's policy of working with Russia was reversed." Roosevelt might have refused to seat Lublin's representatives at San Francisco, and "the strong probability is that he would have, but without telling the Russians to go to hell."[9]

[9] *Cold War*, 266-267.

Turning to the meeting with Molotov, Fleming had the Russian no sooner being "ushered in to pay his respects to the new President" than Truman delivered a humiliating "tongue lashing such as the minister of a Central American republic might bridle under." Citing the later comment of Admiral Leahy (who attended this meeting) that " 'personally I did not believe that the dominating Soviet influence could be excluded from Poland . . . ,' " Fleming made it appear that that was precisely what Truman demanded. When the President "would not concede to Molotov that the interests of Russia in Poland were controlling, . . . the meeting ended abruptly."[10]

Fleming described Truman's conduct in apocalyptic terms. The President was "ready to begin it [the Cold War] before he had been in office two weeks," he "cancelled out" the "years of labor" by Roosevelt and Hull, he was trying to "lay down the law," and he was giving notice that "in areas of most crucial concern to Russia our wishes must be obeyed." Most ominous of all, Truman's performance meant that "the signals [were] set for many years of desperate and dangerous power rivalry, beginning in Eastern Europe and involving the expenditure of many hundreds of billions of dollars in an atomic armament race."[11]

Fleming's presentation of this incident is defective in many respects. He never seemed to get straight in his own mind what role Leahy played. First he had the Admiral almost singlehandedly priming Truman to confront the Russians at the earliest opportunity. When the opportunity presented itself, however, Fleming had Leahy counseling moderation. No reason is given for Leahy's appar-

[10] *Ibid.*, 268.　　　　[11] *Ibid.*, 268-269.

45

ent reversal, nor any hint as to why his influence suddenly vanished at this point. In fact, Fleming misconstrued Leahy's advice at the April 23rd meeting; the Admiral stressed the importance of the situation but urged the President to stand firm.[12]

On a broader level, Fleming's emphasis upon Leahy's briefings during this period, rather than upon Russian actions, made it seem that Truman more or less arbitrarily contrived a "showdown" for no stronger reason than the desire that the Soviet Union be "slapped down, then and there," to use Fleming's words.[13] The facts point to a different conclusion. As far back as the Yalta Conference Roosevelt had informed Stalin that "I have to make it clear to you that we cannot recognize the Lublin Government as now composed. . . ," and his cable to the Russian Premier of April 1 showed that he had not budged from this stand during his last days.[14] Yet, between the time of his death and the date of the Truman–Molotov confrontation, evidence accumulated that the Soviet Union meant to secure the Lublin Government's control over Poland. The Russians had unilaterally turned over to the Lublin Poles a large chunk of German territory (in violation of existing zonal arrangements), had arrested sixteen Polish underground leaders, and had concluded over American protests a mutual defense pact with the Lublin group.[15] All these steps had the effect of consolidating Lublin's position as *the* government of Poland. Now, it appeared to Truman, Stalin intended to force

[12] Truman, *Year of Decisions*, 78.

[13] *Cold War*, 268.   [14] *Yalta Papers*, 728.

[15] Herbert Feis, *Churchill-Roosevelt-Stalin: The War They Waged and the Peace They Sought* (Princeton: Princeton University Press, 1957), 577-580.

46

Anglo-American acquiescence by threatening to boycott the United Nations' founding conference unless Lublin were invited to attend as the legitimate government of Poland.

Truman's "showdown" with Molotov, therefore, stemmed from the former's determination to adhere to Roosevelt's stated position that either the Lublin group or a "thinly disguised continuance" of it was unacceptable to the United States. Since the meeting took place only two days before the conference was scheduled to open, it is difficult to see how the new President could have avoided precipitating some kind of crisis except by compromising his predecessor's policy. It might be argued that Roosevelt was naive in believing that Stalin would accept more than a token reorganization of the Lublin regime. It might also be argued that F.D.R. would have backed off in the face of Russia's determination had he lived. Such speculation should not obscure the fact that Truman incurred the risk he did by hewing to, not by departing from, Roosevelt's interpretation of the Yalta agreement on Poland.

Against this background, Truman's remark to his aides about his determination "to go on with the plans for San Francisco" was not as pugnacious as Fleming made it appear. The President in effect was saying that he would not retreat from the American position as stated repeatedly by Roosevelt, and that the next move would be up to the Russians. It need hardly be added that Fleming's comment that Roosevelt would not have told the Russians "they could go to hell" is gratuitous; Truman used that expression in the presence of his advisors, not in his talk with Molotov.

47

Fleming's description of the Truman–Molotov meeting itself is just as misleading. Molotov was not there to "pay his respects to the new President"; he had completed that formality the day before. He was there to discuss the Polish question, and both men knew from talks the Russian had had with Stettinius and British Foreign Minister Anthony Eden over the previous two days that their positions were irreconcilable unless one or the other backed down.[16] Fleming's allegation that the meeting ended abruptly when Truman "would not concede to Molotov that the interests of Russia in Poland were controlling," furthermore, blurred the President's actual stance. A week earlier he and Churchill had forwarded to Stalin a joint message suggesting ways the Churchill–Roosevelt proposals of April 1 could be implemented. In this second communiqué they reminded Stalin that "we have never denied that among the three elements from which the new Provisional Government of National Unity is to be formed the representatives of the present Warsaw [Lublin] Government will play, unquestionably, a prominent part."[17] Truman informed Molotov that he and Churchill had "gone as far as we could" in this message. In short, he refused to retreat from Roosevelt's unwillingness either to recognize Lublin as the legal government of Poland or to accord to it the right to determine which Poles would participate in the formation of a new government.

What, then, is left of Fleming's thesis about a "sudden reversal" of Roosevelt's policies? That Truman used undiplomatic language during the course of his talk with Mol-

[16] Truman, *Year of Decisions*, 75-77.
[17] *Ibid.*, 38.

otov is beyond dispute. Presumably Roosevelt would have stated his case in a more diplomatic fashion, although he too had expressed exasperation over Russia's actions in behalf of the Lublin group. Had he abided by his previous declarations, however, the substance of what he would have told Molotov would have been equally displeasing to the Soviets. Fleming also ignored the fact that toward the end of the meeting Truman handed Molotov a message to be communicated to Stalin in which the President "earnestly" requested that the Soviet Union agree to the suggestions he and Churchill had forwarded, and urged the Premier to permit Molotov to continue the conversations over Poland at the San Francisco Conference. Although Truman warned Stalin that the failure to make progress on the Polish question would " 'seriously shake confidence in the unity of the three governments,' " he mentioned no time limits.[18] Negotiations did in fact continue at San Francisco, and Fleming adduced no evidence to show that the Russians interpreted Truman's behavior as having closed the door to accommodation.

Nor was the door closed. Less than three months after the Truman–Molotov meeting the United States extended recognition to a Polish government which turned out to be little more than the "thinly disguised continuance" of the Lublin regime Roosevelt had warned against. Fleming's discussion of that event showed remarkable restraint when compared with the purple prose he lavished on the Truman–Molotov session. "On July 5 Secretary of State Byrnes recognized the Provisional Government of National Unity," he wrote, "and withdrew recognition from the London Polish Government."[19] Nothing more. There

[18] *Ibid.*, 80-81.   [19] *Cold War*, 240.

is no hint that this step represented a concession on Truman's part, nor any explanation of why a man so bent upon launching the Cold War would have taken it.

Fleming's use of language throughout his discussion of this incident is characteristic of the double-standard he applied to Russia and the United States. The Russians claimed that the wording of the Yalta agreement gave the Lublin group the right to choose which Poles could participate in consultations; the United States claimed that it did not. When referring to the Soviet position, Fleming merely stated it as an interpretation of the Yalta accord. The American construction of the agreement, however, amounted to "lay[ing] down the law" or insisting that its "wishes must be obeyed."[20] One could just as easily transpose these phrases and have the Americans interpreting the document while the Russians laid down the law.

Fleming's justification for the Russian interpretation is interesting, too. As Roosevelt himself pointed out, there was nothing in the recorded discussions at Yalta, or in the text of the protocol, to indicate that the signatories thought they were granting to the Lublin group the right of veto. To Fleming there was. "The Yalta agreement said that the Allied Commission for Poland," he wrote, "would consult *in the first instance* with members of the existing 'Provisional Government and with other Polish Democratic leaders from within Poland and from abroad.' "[21] That is incorrect. What it said was that the Commission would "consult *in the first instance in Moscow* with members of the present Provisional Govern-

[20] *Ibid.*, 268, 269.
[21] *Ibid.*, 211 (Fleming's emphasis).

ment. . . ."[22] In other words, Fleming misplaced the phrase "in the first instance," thereby making it appear that the sentence referred to the *order* in which groups would be consulted rather than the *place* where the first deliberations would be held.

Despite his charge that Truman was prepared to touch off the Cold War "from the eminence of eleven days in power,"[23] Fleming's treatment of the President's conduct from that point until the Potsdam Conference is ambivalent. He cited a number of examples to demonstrate Truman's bellicosity, and at the same time credited the President with genuine efforts to reach some sort of working arrangement with the Russians. Truman's decision in May to send Harry Hopkins to negotiate with Stalin over the Polish question provides a case in point. Unlike some of the later revisionists, who would interpret the Hopkins mission as no more than a ruse on Truman's part, Fleming did not impugn the President's sincerity on this matter.[24] He severely criticized many aspects of American diplomacy as manifested at Potsdam, yet concluded that "a good foundation for further Allied collaboration was laid down" there.[25] At that very moment, according to Fleming, American officials decided to undermine the foundation. Their new calculations were based on the knowledge that within weeks the United States would possess nuclear weapons.

The United States dropped the atomic bombs on Japan for a number of reasons, in Fleming's view, among them the desire to save lives and to avoid an immense re-

[22] *Yalta Papers*, 980 (emphasis added).
[23] *Cold War*, 268.   [24] *Ibid.*, 238-239.   [25] *Ibid.*, 294.

deployment of forces. These factors alone "made the military use of the A-bomb more than likely."[26] As to timing, however, he posited one overriding motive: the wish to defeat Japan before the Soviet Union could declare war against her so as to minimize the expansion of Russian power in the Far East. This decision had far-reaching consequences, for it "definitely marked the end of the war-time alliance with the Soviet Union and the beginning of the post-war balance of power struggle."[27]

The cornerstone of Fleming's interpretation is his assumption about the date American officials believed Russia would enter the war in the Pacific. That day, August 8, is presented in *The Cold War and Its Origins* as the deadline against which Truman and his advisors worked. The President's decision to issue to Japan a warning and call to surrender on July 26, while the Potsdam Conference sat, derived from his wish to exclude the Soviet Union from the anti-Japanese coalition. Not that the Americans thought the warning itself would bring results. Quite the opposite. Assuming that the Japanese would reject the proclamation, American policymakers saw as its real purpose giving them the excuse to proceed quickly with the atomic attack. That action, they believed, would force Japan's capitulation before Russia could play any meaningful role in the Far Eastern war.[28]

Like William Appleman Williams in *The Tragedy of American Diplomacy*, Fleming attached a great deal of importance to Secretary of War Henry L. Stimson's memorandum to Truman of July 2. In that document, it will be recalled, Stimson proposed warning the Japanese "of

[26] *Ibid.*, 298.   [27] *Ibid.*, 308.   [28] *Ibid.*, 302-303.

the inevitability and completeness of the destruction" which could be visited upon them should they refuse to surrender. "If Russia is a part of the threat," Stimson wrote in one passage, "the Russian attack, if actual, must not have progressed too far."[29] To Fleming, this statement meant that "effective use of the bomb depended either on dropping it before Russia's entry into the war or immediately afterwards." Truman accepted Stimson's assessment of the situation, according to Fleming, and "decided to try to force Japan's surrender by A-bomb attack before Russia's entry into the war on August 8."[30]

A number of errors mar Fleming's thesis. The most important is his assertion that administration officials knew Russia intended to declare war on August 8. Because Stalin at Yalta had promised to enter the conflict three months after V-E Day, and because Russia in fact did announce on August 8 (three months to the day after Germany's surrender) that she would declare war, his conclusion seems eminently plausible. It is mistaken. The point Fleming ignored was that Stalin qualified his pledge with the proviso that negotiations between the Soviet Union and China had to be completed before he would act. He and Molotov restated this position several times at Potsdam in conversations with American officials.[31]

The prospects for an early Sino-Soviet agreement appeared dim. Negotiations between the two powers had been suspended at the time of Potsdam, and Chiang Kai-

[29] Stimson and Bundy, *On Active Service*, 620-624.

[30] *Cold War*, 302.

[31] Herbert Feis, *Between War and Peace: The Potsdam Conference* (Princeton: Princeton University Press, 1960), 113; Byrnes, *All in One Lifetime*, 290-291; Truman, *Year of Decisions*, 401.

shek's government had indicated its belief that Stalin's proposed terms exceeded the agreements made at Yalta. Indeed, the very fact that the United States at this time notified China that it would not ask her to concede more than the Yalta accords called for has been presented by some revisionists—though not Fleming—as evidence that Truman thereby hoped to delay Russian entry for as long as possible.[32] Given Stalin's stated conditions, American officials had no reason to believe August 8 constituted any deadline. Unless the Russian leader deliberately misled his American counterparts, moreover, it seems certain that the bombing of Hiroshima caused Russia to act when she did, rather than did the fore-knowledge of that act dictate the bomb's use.

Fleming also erred in his use of the Stimson memorandum. The Secretary's point about a Russian attack not having "progressed too far" was made within the context of the timing of the proposed warning, not the timing of an atomic attack. This is made clear by his preceding comments:

> She [Japan] has an extremely sensitive national pride, and, as we are now seeing every day, when actually

[32] On July 23 Truman telegraphed Chiang Kai-shek from Potsdam: " 'I asked that you carry out the Yalta agreement, but I had not asked that you make any concession in excess of that agreement. If you and Generalissimo Stalin differ as to the correct interpretation of the Yalta agreement, I hope you will arrange for [T.V.] Soong to return to Moscow and continue your efforts to reach complete understanding.' " Truman, *Year of Decisions*, 320. For the allegation that Truman wished to forestall a Sino-Russian agreement, see Gar Alperovitz, *Atomic Diplomacy: Hiroshima and Potsdam, The Use of the Atomic Bomb and The American Confrontation with Soviet Power* (New York: Simon and Schuster, 1965), 183-184.

locked with the enemy will fight to the very death. For that reason the warning must be tendered before the actual invasion has occurred and while the impending destruction, though clear beyond peradventure, has not yet reduced her to fanatical despair. If Russia is a part of the threat the Russian attack . . . .[33]

Indeed, Stimson's memorandum did not even mention the atomic bomb.

As further evidence that the United States by the time of the Potsdam Conference wished to exclude the Soviet Union from the war against Japan, Fleming wrote:

Two days later [July 29] Molotov came to arrange the immediate occasion of Russia's entry into the war. Wouldn't the Allies invite Russia in! This presented "a problem to us" which it took hours to solve. The President was "disturbed" and, because of Soviet acts in East Europe since Yalta, Byrnes would have been "satisfied" had the Russians decided not to enter the war.[34]

Fleming's version of the situation made it appear that the Soviet desire to enter the war quickly (perhaps even before the 8th) was what presented "a problem," which "disturbed" Truman and took "hours" to solve. But the source for his analysis, Byrnes's *Speaking Frankly*, did not mention any sense of urgency on the part of the Soviet Union. The "immediate occasion" ("immediate cause," as Byrnes put it) in context meant simply the formal justification for Russia's entry.[35] Molotov told Byrnes at the time "that the Soviet Government was assuming, of course, that the agreement with the Chinese

[33] Stimson and Bundy, *On Active Service*, 624.
[34] *Cold War*, 303.
[35] Byrnes, *Speaking Frankly*, 207.

Government would be signed before his country entered the war."[36] Since negotiations toward that end were not even going on then, the "hours" it took to formulate a reply had no significance whatever.

Fleming's disarming "Wouldn't the Allies invite Russia in!" is similarly deceptive, suggesting as it does a vision of Molotov deferentially tugging his forelock, had one existed. But the issue was not whether the Allies would indicate they desired Russian participation, for they had done so repeatedly. It was that the Soviet Union had asked them to make a formal request to that effect. As the Russo-Japanese nonaggression pact still obtained (and had almost a year to run), such a request would have placed upon the United States the onus of publicly asking another nation to violate its treaty commitments. This was what presented a "problem," according to Byrnes, and "disturbed" Truman. Instead, Byrnes and an aide drafted a note to Stalin suggesting that he base Russian entry upon the obligations assumed by the Moscow Declaration of October 30, 1943, and upon certain provisions of the as yet unratified United Nations Charter. Truman forwarded the message immediately, and later told Byrnes that Stalin "expressed great appreciation of the communication."[37]

The destruction visited upon Hiroshima and Nagasaki, according to Fleming, had immediate and catastrophic effects on relations with the Soviet Union. The new weapon's existence (and, to Russia, the fact that the United States had used it) caused both nations to become even more determined to achieve their goals, at whatever cost. Fleming put it this way:

[36] *Ibid.*, 207.   [37] *Ibid.*, 208-209.

Up to this time control of Eastern Europe had seemed vital to them [the Russians] as a means of preventing a German come-back. Now the same region was even more vital as a buffer against the atomic-armed West.

On its side the West now decided to act strongly to secure "free and unfettered elections" in the Balkans.[38]

When, even before Japan surrendered, Truman opened a "diplomatic offensive" by stating on August 9 that Rumania, Bulgaria, and Hungary were " 'not to be spheres of influence of any one power,' " he served notice that the United States meant to exploit its recently achieved power. But the Russians, uncowed by the bomb, refused to knuckle under. They left no doubt of that fact in September at the first meeting of the Council of Foreign Ministers: Molotov caused the meeting to adjourn without agreement by refusing to accept American proposals on Bulgaria and Rumania. Instead of conceding to Russia what he must have known she deemed vital for her own security, Truman within weeks "began composing the Truman Doctrine for the 'containment' of the Soviet Union." The Cold War, if yet undeclared, had already begun.[39]

Fleming's presentation of the "diplomatic offensive" and its consequences closely resembles his handling of events previously discussed in this essay. A few examples must suffice. He cited Truman's August 9 statement that Rumania, Bulgaria, and Hungary were " 'not to be spheres of influence of any one power' " as though the President intended this as a challenge to the Soviet Union. Perhaps he did, but when placed in its proper context the

[38] *Cold War*, 308.
[39] *Ibid.*, 268-269, 309-310, 311-314, 333.

phrase appears far more innocuous than Fleming would have it. Truman was reporting to the American people the results of the Potsdam Conference. He was generous to the Soviet Union ("In the conference of Berlin it was easy for me to get along in mutual understanding and friendship with Generalissimo Stalin. . ."), and his "spheres of influence" phrase appeared in a passage devoted to decisions reached among the Big Three. At Yalta, he said, it had been agreed that the three powers had a "common responsibility" for liberated and (German) satellite states. He continued:

> That responsibility still stands. We all recognize it as a joint responsibility of the three governments.
>
> It was reaffirmed in the Berlin declaration on Rumania, Bulgaria, and Hungary. These nations are not to be spheres of influence of any one power.[40]

Nowhere in his discussion either of Potsdam or of the "diplomatic offensive" did Fleming even so much as hint that there was any such agreement.[41] As where Poland was concerned, it may have been advisable for the United States to have backed off subsequently, in the face of Russian intransigence, but that is another matter.

Fleming borrowed the phrase "diplomatic offensive" from one *New York Times* columnist (C. L. Sulzburger) and depended upon another for his conclusion regarding the consequences of its failure.[42] Fleming's source for his claim that the "Truman Doctrine" had "matured" in the President's mind by mid-November 1945 was a column

[40] *New York Times*, August 10, 1945, p. 12, col. 5.

[41] See Feis, *Between War and Peace*, 350-351, for text of the Potsdam agreement on Rumania, Bulgaria, and Hungary.

[42] *New York Times*, August 26, 1945, p. E5, col. 6.

58

Arthur Krock wrote in 1947.[43] Krock actually said only that there "is good reason to believe" such was the case, but Fleming, pronouncing the article "authoritative," converted the reporter's estimate into a statement of fact. He distorted the sense of the column in the bargain, for Krock did not attribute Truman's attitude to the failure of any American offensive. On the contrary, he ascribed it to Truman's growing doubt that a policy of "continued appeasement" towards Russia would achieve peace and security. To Fleming, apparently, only those portions of Krock's column congenial to his own theme were authoritative.

The Krock column, Edgar Snow's interview with F.D.R., and the *Colliers* article typify the heavy reliance placed upon journalistic sources throughout *The Cold War and Its Origins*. It is significant to note the manner in which Fleming used them. Time after time he substantiated one point or another by substituting for evidence (or his own analysis) the opinion of some journalist with whose views he agreed. The individuals he cited were invariably identified as "one of the most responsible correspondents in the capital," "one of the keenest and most penetrating writers of the time," "a keen analyst," or "a noted foreign expert." Their analyses, of course, were "carefully reasoned," "astute," or "objective." Writers with opposing views, on the other hand, were either "hysterical" or merely "cold warriors."[44] It is all very well to cite the opinions of others to support an interpretation, but Fleming often used them as though they constituted

[43] *Ibid.*, March 23, 1947, p. E3, cols. 1 and 2.
[44] For these and similar descriptions, see *Cold War*, 243, 254, 255, 256, 282, 283, 286, 312, 313.

proof in and of themselves. One opinion does not verify another, however; together they add up to two opinions.

Fleming showed himself equally willing to accept on faith Stalin's words. Whereas he usually analyzed the statements of American leaders within the context of their actions (rightly so, whether or not one agrees with his conclusions), he exhibited a trust in Stalin that can only be described as touching. In a section devoted to the Polish question entitled "Was Stalin Insincere at Yalta?", Fleming asserted that as late as June 1945 Stalin had no intention of forcing communism on Poland. His evidence is that Stalin said so to a noncommunist Polish leader in November 1944 and told Harry Hopkins substantially the same thing six months later. Regarding the latter discussion with "his [Stalin's] friend Hopkins," Fleming wrote that Stalin's remarks should be believed because "Hopkins was the man in all the West whom Stalin had most reason to trust, and least reason to hoodwink."[45] Perhaps. But those heads of state who have permitted personal feelings (assuming Stalin thought of Hopkins as "his friend") to stand in the way of what they defined as national interests have been very few, and Stalin's record scarcely lends credence to the assumption that he was one of the exceptions. Fleming's "evidence" is no evidence at all unless one can imagine the alternative: Stalin admitting to Hopkins that he *had* been insincere at Yalta and, furthermore, that he intended to renege on whatever agreements over Poland the two of them reached.

Fleming's book is the cry of a genuinely outraged man. He lived through two world wars, and at the end of both

[45] *Ibid.*, 244-245.

60

he saw the hopes for lasting peace dashed upon the rocks of national hatreds, mutual suspicions, and ideological crusades. But outrage and compassion for suffering mankind do not necessarily produce sound historical analysis. His writing is shot through with factual errors, it is based heavily upon the day-to-day ephemera of reporters laboring under deadlines, and its biases show on every page. It is, in short, unreliable as a scholarly work.

3.

ATOMIC DIPLOMACY: GAR ALPEROVITZ

Iɴ 1965 Gar Alperovitz published *Atomic Diplomacy: Hiroshima and Potsdam, The Use of the Atomic Bomb and the American Confrontation with Soviet Power*, a dramatically revisionist essay on the origins of the Cold War.[1] Since then his book has become a staple of "New Left" historiography; portions of it can be found in the most popular anthologies, and even those "orthodox" historians who do not accept its conclusions generally have treated the work as a scholarly enterprise.[2] *Atomic*

[1] (New York: Simon and Schuster, 1965.)
[2] For "New Left" estimates of the impact Alperovitz and other revisionists have had on interpreting the Cold War, see Christopher Lasch, "The Cold War: Revisited and Re-visioned," *New York Times Magazine*, January 14, 1968, and Walter La-Feber "War: Cold," *Cornell Alumni News* 71 (October 1968). Excerpts from LaFeber's article are reprinted in Thomas G. Paterson (ed.), *The Origins of the Cold War* (Lexington, Mass.: D. C. Heath, 1970), 118-120. Paterson's volume, one of the *Problems in American Civilization* series, contains most of the concluding chapters of *Atomic Diplomacy* as presented in an earlier form, 30-35. Selections from Alperovitz's book can also be found in Paul R. Baker (ed.), *The Atomic Bomb: The Great Decision* (New York: Holt, Rinehart and Winston, 1968), 58-64; and William A. Williams, *The Shaping of American Diplomacy, II* (2nd edn., Chicago: Rand McNally, 1970), 358-365. For an "orthodox" assessment of *Atomic Diplomacy*, see Norman A. Graebner, "Cold War Origins and the Contemporary Debate: A Review of Recent Literature," *Journal of Conflict Resolution*

Diplomacy, Christopher Lasch has proclaimed, "made it difficult for conscientious scholars any longer to avoid the challenge of revisionist interpretations."[3] That orthodox historians have not responded more vigorously to revisionism as exemplified by *Atomic Diplomacy* is surprising, for an examination of the sources upon which it is based reveals that the book is unable to withstand scrutiny.

The bulk of Alperovitz's work is devoted to showing that from the time Harry S Truman assumed the presidency he undertook to reverse Franklin D. Roosevelt's policy of cooperation with the Soviet Union, thereby precipitating the Cold War. In direct violation of wartime agreements, some explicit and some understood, Truman sought to construct an American-dominated world order (particularly in Eastern Europe and the Far East) at the end of World War II. When economic coercion failed to achieve this goal, Alperovitz claimed, Truman bided his time until the United States acquired the atomic bomb, with which he meant to cow the Russians into submission. The use of nuclear weapons against an already defeated Japan, according to this view, amounted to a diplomatic rather than a military act. The evidence

---

XIII (March 1969), 123-132. Even those orthodox historians who criticized *Atomic Diplomacy* most severely did so on the ground that Alperovitz had not presented sufficient evidence to validate his theses. An exception is Arthur Schlesinger, jr., who wrote of Alperovitz that "he sometimes twists his material in a most unscholarly way," in *The Crisis of Confidence* (New York: Bantam, 1969), 79. Schlesinger cited three examples of how Alperovitz misused his sources, one of which is reproduced below.

[3] See his Introduction to Gar Alperovitz, *Cold War Essays* (New York: Doubleday, 1970), 12.

"strongly suggests," he wrote, that the bombs were used primarily to demonstrate to the Russians the enormous power America would have in its possession during subsequent negotiations.[4] As a lesser factor, he cited the wish to end the war quickly before they could establish a strong position in the Far East. Although denying that he intended to present a systematic analysis of Soviet diplomacy, Alperovitz depicted Stalin as merely trying to attain for the Soviet Union its legitimate security needs in the face of increasing American militance.

One of the most common flaws in the book is Alperovitz's practice of citing statements in support of his arguments which, in context, refer to other subjects altogether. The opening paragraph of his first chapter is typical:

> Only eleven days had passed since the death of Franklin Delano Roosevelt. The new President of the United States prepared for his first meeting with a representative of the Soviet Union. Rehearsing his views on the subject of the negotiation—a reorganization of the Polish government—Truman declared that if the Russians did not care to cooperate, "they could go to hell."[5]

The quotation, from Charles E. Bohlen's notes of the conversation, is cited correctly, but applied to the wrong issue. In context Truman was referring to the possibility that the Russians might boycott the founding conference of the United Nations if they did not get *their* way on

---

[4] *Atomic Diplomacy*, 242. Although Williams and Fleming (and P.M.S. Blackett before them) had argued essentially the same thesis, *Atomic Diplomacy* is the first full-length study devoted to this issue.

[5] *Ibid.*, 19.

Poland. "He intended to go on with the plans for San Francisco," Bohlen reported him as saying, "and if the Russians did not wish to join us they could go to hell. . . ."[6] Alperovitz's version helps establish Truman's intransigency on the Polish question, but it is incorrect.

Contending that American policymakers at an early date meant to influence events in Eastern Europe "behind Red Army lines," to cite another example, Alperovitz wrote that "what went on in the liberated areas had already been defined as 'of urgent importance to the U. S.' by the time Truman took office."[7] His source for this quotation is a State Department position paper, reprinted in Truman's *Year of Decisions*. The words are taken from the first sentence of a paragraph headed SUPPLIES FOR LIBERATED AREAS, and the entire sentence reads: "A problem of urgent importance to the U. S. is that of supplies for areas liberated from enemy occupation."[8] Since the point was made earlier in the paper that "in the liberated areas under Soviet control, the Soviet Government is proceeding largely on a unilateral basis . . . ," it seems almost certain that the passage in question has to do with administering regions captured by Western armies.[9] Yet, in Alperovitz's hands, it became an expression of intended interference in Soviet-held territory.

In developing his thesis that Truman initially seized upon economic leverage to gain his ends in Eastern Europe, Alperovitz again used words having to do with one

[6] Walter Millis and E. S. Duffield (eds.), *The Forrestal Diaries* (New York: Viking, 1951), 50.

[7] *Atomic Diplomacy*, 25.   [8] *Year of Decisions*, 17.

[9] *Ibid.*, 15.

subject to apply to another. He assigned to W. Averell Harriman, then Ambassador to Russia, a great deal of influence in converting Truman to this project. In his discussion of alleged debates over curtailing Lend-Lease aid as a primary tool, Alperovitz quoted Harriman as arguing that the United States " 'should retain current control of . . . credits [to the Russians] in order to be in a position to protect American vital interests in the formulative period immediately following the war.' "[10] A look at the source for this remark, however, reveals that Harriman's statement did not pertain to Lend Lease at all, but to postwar dollar credits. Alperovitz's excision of the word "these" ("these credits") gave the sentence a meaning Harriman never intended.[11]

Time sequences fared as badly in *Atomic Diplomacy* as did subject matter. At the conclusion of the paragraph containing Harriman's altered sentence (a paragraph dealing with events in April–May 1945), Alperovitz cited General John R. Deane, Chief of the United States Military Mission in Moscow, to show what American leaders believed Lend-Lease curtailment would accomplish: "This would increase America's economic leverage and would 'make the Soviet authorities come to us,' as Deane had phrased it."[12] Actually, Deane's phrase appeared in a letter he wrote to General George C. Marshall *in December 1944*, months before the so-called debates took place. What Deane really said is of interest, too: "We should stop pushing ourselves on them and make the Soviet authorities come to us. We should be friendly and

[10] *Atomic Diplomacy*, 35.   [11] *Forrestal Diaries*, 41.
[12] *Atomic Diplomacy*, 36.

co-operative when they do so."[13] This hardly amounts to a recipe for coercion.

Another example of faulty chronology can be found in Alperovitz's analysis of what American leaders believed possession of atomic weapons would enable them to extract from the Russians. In the context of post-Alamagordo appraisals of the possibilities, Alperovitz cited as Secretary of State James F. Byrnes's "new advice" to Truman that " 'the bomb might well put us in a position to dictate our own terms. . . .' "[14] The words attributed to Byrnes were what Truman recalled him as having said in April 1945. And Alperovitz's omission of the latter part of Byrnes's statement, "at the end of the war," is misleading, to say the least. As Truman's prose makes plain, the statement he ascribed to Byrnes referred to terms with *Japan* "at the end of the war," not terms with Russia after it.[15]

Indeed, Alperovitz's use of hiatuses in *Atomic Diplomacy* often resulted in discrepancies of the gravest kind. Assessing the significance of Hiroshima and Nagasaki, Alperovitz wrote that "Truman has characterized the result: 'Our dropping of the atomic bomb on Japan . . . forced Russia to reconsider her position in the Far East.' "[16] Here he omitted the word "had" which, if left

[13] John R. Deane, *The Strange Alliance: The Story of Our Efforts at Wartime Co-operation with Russia* (New York: Viking, 1947), 86.

[14] *Atomic Diplomacy*, 229.

[15] *Year of Decisions*, 87. Truman's next sentence reads: "Stimson, on the other hand, seemed at least as much concerned with the role of the atomic bomb in the shaping of history as in its capacity to shorten this war." This would make it seem obvious that Byrnes's statement had referred to shortening the war.

[16] *Atomic Diplomacy*, 191.

in, might have suggested what Truman actually was referring to: Russia's decision to join the war against Japan
as soon as she did (even though certain preconditions
had yet to be fulfilled) rather than her behavior vis-à-vis
the United States after the war ended. "Without warning,
while Russian–Chinese negotiations were still far from
agreement," Truman had written, "Molotov sent for Ambassador Harriman on August 8 and announced to him
that the Soviet Union would consider itself at war with
Japan as of August 9. This move did not surprise us.
Our dropping of the atomic bomb on Japan had forced
Russia to reconsider her position in the Far East."[17]

Often Alperovitz pared remarks in such a way as to
render them inappropriate to the context in which he
presented them. In a chapter entitled "The Decision to
Postpone a Confrontation with Stalin," he tried to show
that Truman's refusal to attend a meeting of the Big
Three before July 1945 was part of an agreed-upon strategy to hold off a showdown with the Russians until the
United States had the nuclear bomb to shake at them. Admitting that he could find no direct evidence for this
theory, Alperovitz sought to build a circumstantial case
by belittling Truman's announced reasons. He quoted the
President as having refused to attend solely on the ground
that he had to prepare a "budget message," which excuse
Alperovitz disparaged as "impossibly weak."[18] In fact,
Truman said he had to contend with "a number of pressing domestic questions," the budget message "particularly" because the fiscal year was coming to an end.[19]

[17] *Year of Decisions*, 425.   [18] *Atomic Diplomacy*, 67.
[19] *Potsdam Papers* I, 13. And, as one might expect, the preparation of a budget message depended upon the preparation of a

69

Alperovitz's need to establish that a "strategy" existed is crucial to his theme, for it enabled him to argue that seemingly conciliatory moves by Truman—such as sending Harry Hopkins to Moscow—were but cynical steps in the grand design.[20]

---

budget. "This was to be my first budget as President," Truman later wrote, "and I hoped to be able to justify every detail it contained" (*Year of Decisions*, 99). That the problems of converting to a peacetime economy did comprise one of Truman's larger concerns can be seen in his *Year of Decisions*, 58-59, 95-99, 226-227. Truman explained in some detail the problems involved to Anthony Eden and other British leaders only a week after Winston Churchill first suggested a meeting. See *Potsdam Papers* I, 11.

[20] There is evidence to show that when Truman, on May 28, asked that the meeting date be changed from "early" July (the time he suggested in response to Churchill's inquiry) to the 15th of July, he had the atomic tests in mind. See Richard G. Hewlett and Oscar E. Anderson, Jr., *A History of the United States Atomic Energy Commission, Volume I: The New World, 1939-1946* (University Park: The Pennsylvania State University Press, 1962), 352. This date, however, is far too late to support Alperovitz's "strategy" thesis. Actually, Alperovitz's chronology is quite muddled through the first three chapters. In Chapter I, "The Strategy of an Immediate Showdown," he argued that the chief component of this strategy was curtailment of Lend-Lease aid. Truman's memorandum ordering the cutback was issued May 11, 1945. In Chapter II, "The Strategy of a Delayed Showdown," and in Chapter III, Alperovitz contended that the President, sometime between late April and early May, decided to postpone a showdown with Stalin until the United States had obtained the bomb. In an appendix Alperovitz estimated the date of this decision as April 25, *more than two weeks before* the curtailment of Lend Lease. He tried to explain this discrepancy with the comment that Truman "held on to his firm line of policy while he secretly prepared his new approach" (*Atomic Diplomacy*, 272). If true, Truman guarded his secret well, for no evidence has yet surfaced to show that he was preparing a new approach. For an

From the Henry L. Stimson diaries, Alperovitz has the then Secretary of War on May 14, 1945, discussing "the role of the bomb and European diplomacy with British Foreign Secretary Anthony Eden, outlining 'to him the progress which we have made and the timetable as it stood now, and . . . its bearing upon our present problems of an international character.' "[21] A bit later in the book, using the same diary entry as his source, Alperovitz construed this as "explained the role of the atomic bomb" and, further on, declared that Stimson "appears" to have "confidentially delineated the more sophisticated strategy" (that of delaying a showdown until the bomb was ready) to Eden.[22] Thus Stimson's reference to the bomb expands from its "bearing" on problems, to its "role" in American policy, to its part in "the more sophisticated strategy" Truman had adopted. When the words replaced by the hiatus are supplied to Stimson's diary entry, however, it becomes clear that the cited passage supports none of these constructions. What Stimson wrote was that he had "told him [Eden] of my own feelings as to" the bomb's bearing on problems.[23] The phrase "my own feelings" makes it seem obvious that he conveyed to Eden no administration decisions of any kind.

---

effective rebuttal of the notion that Lend-Lease curtailment was designed to coerce Russia, see George C. Herring, Jr., "Lend Lease to Russia and the Origins of the Cold War, 1944-1945," *The Journal of American History* LVI (June 1969), 93-114.

[21] *Atomic Diplomacy*, 58.

[22] *Ibid.*, 60, 67.

[23] Henry L. Stimson *Diary*, entry dated May 14, 1945, Yale University Library, New Haven, Connecticut. In an appendix Alperovitz cited the statement again, this time with the missing words supplied (see 271).

Another instance of this practice can be seen in the author's conclusions about Truman's overall conduct toward the Soviet Union. "The President's attitude," he wrote, "is best summed up in the statement he made eight days after Roosevelt's death. He 'intended to be firm with the Russians and make no concessions.' "[24] The latter part of the quoted sentence, which Alperovitz left out, reads: "from American principles or traditions in order to win their favor." Truman did not say that he would make "no concessions" and, in the same paragraph, he alluded to the need for establishing relations on "a give-and-take basis."[25]

Perhaps the most amusing illustration of this kind occurred in Alperovitz's efforts to show Truman's disappointment at learning that technical difficulties would postpone the nuclear test until after the Potsdam meeting had begun. Referring to the President's state of mind at that time, Alperovitz wrote that "Truman made no attempt to hide his feelings: 'I am getting ready to go see Stalin and Churchill, and it is a chore. . . .Wish I didn't have to go, but I do, and it can't be stopped now.' "[26] Again the hiatus produced a most serious distortion, this time replacing "I have to take my tuxedo, tails . . . preacher coat, high hat, low hat and hard hat as well as sundry other things," and another sentence in the same vein.[27] What Alperovitz presented as the words of President Truman, global strategist, turns out to be Ol' Cap'n Harry, complaining to "Momma and Mary" about the formalities he would have to endure.

[24] *Atomic Diplomacy*, 231.   [25] *Year of Decisions*, 71.
[26] *Atomic Diplomacy*, 145.
[27] *Year of Decisions*, 331 (Truman's ellipsis).

The heaviest concentration of misrendered sources appears in Alperovitz's account of how Americans assessed political conditions in Eastern Europe by mid-1945. Because it is central to his theme that Truman, not Stalin, meant to renege on previous agreements, Alperovitz went to great lengths to show that on balance Stalin lived up to understandings reached at Yalta and elsewhere. In his passages on the situation in Hungary as of July 1945, for instance, Alperovitz cited a State Department Briefing Book Paper as having reported that "power was exercised by 'a coalition government headed by a conservative general [which] includes representatives of the five principal parties of the center and the left. . . . There has been no attempt . . . to substitute a purely leftist regime for the present coalition government.' "[28] That is not what the paper said. The quoted description of the coalition government is transcribed correctly, but the point made in the paper is that the coalition government did *not* exercise power. "Real political power," it said, "resides not in the cabinet or the assembly but in the party organizations and leaders, of whom the Communists, encouraged by the presence of the Red Army, are the strongest."[29] Alperovitz's statement that "the State Department believed that Communist political strength was increasing due to the presence of the Red Army" mitigated but did not compensate for this distortion.

Reports on conditions in Bulgaria, as they appear in *Atomic Diplomacy*, yield similar infidelities. Writing of the "Fatherland Front" government under Colonel Kimon Georgiev, Alperovitz quoted the State Department representative in Bulgaria as having described Georgiev

[28] *Atomic Diplomacy*, 139.   [29] *Potsdam Papers* I, 369-370.

as " 'a true conservative in his views of the sacredness of private property (otherwise he could never have held highest political office in country). . . .' "[30] Omitted from this sentence is the first word "While" ("While a true conservative") and the latter half, which reads: "he is a Simon pure totalitarian when it comes to party govt and state control of private initiative." Because of this and other observations along the same lines, the report's author declared that it "is not unnatural that he should be prepared to go along with Communists who want to take country full way along Soviet road and who will never be content merely with a permanent pro-Soviet orientation of Bulgarian foreign policy."[31] As with Hungary, Alperovitz did not question the accuracy of the reports, he simply misrepresented what they contained.

Such examples can be found throughout the pages of *Atomic Diplomacy.* From an Assistant Secretary of the Navy's memorandum of a cabinet meeting, Alperovitz quoted Roosevelt as having said, among other things, that the British were "perfectly willing" for the United States to go to war with the Soviet Union, without mentioning the Secretary's observation that F.D.R. spoke in "a semi-jocular manner."[32] Elsewhere, referring to Truman's confidence in "the strength economic aid gave to America's bargaining position" and to his belief that "there was not much danger of a break" over the use of this lever, Alperovitz has the President prepared to let Soviet Foreign Minister Vyacheslav M. Molotov know

[30] *Atomic Diplomacy*, 206.   [31] *Potsdam Papers* II, 729.
[32] *Atomic Diplomacy*, 253. For the entire memorandum, see *Forrestal Diaries*, 36-37.

of these feelings " 'in words of one syllable.' "[33] What Truman actually intended to let Molotov know of "in words of one syllable" was his belief that "unless settlement of the Polish question was achieved along the lines of the Crimea decision, the treaty of American adherence to a world organization would not get through the Senate."[34] This is a rather different matter.

Just as he excluded from statements those words or phrases which did not support his themes, Alperovitz often endowed quotations with inferences which are not justified by the sources. Witness his dramatic description of the days between Russia's declaration of war on Japan and the Japanese surrender: "Aware that each hour meant a further advance of the Soviet armies, and also some loss of life, American leaders now became extremely impatient. 'Never have I known time to pass so slowly,' Byrnes recalls."[35] What Byrnes recalled was that "There was little doubt that the Japanese government would respond favorably [to surrender terms], but meanwhile the war went on and every hour meant a tragic waste of life. Never have I known time to pass so slowly."[36] His comment applied solely to the "tragic waste of life"; nowhere in this passage does he indicate that advancing Red armies had anything to do with his emotional state.

Another instance of burdening words with imports not found in the documents can be seen in Alperovitz's assessment of the "Atomic Diplomacy" inaugurated after Hiroshima and Nagasaki. "American diplomacy changed

[33] *Atomic Diplomacy*, 29.   [34] *Year of Decisions*, 71-72.
[35] *Atomic Diplomacy*, 191.   [36] *All in One Lifetime*, 306.

so swiftly that few observers have caught the sweep of all the policy decisions unveiled in a few short weeks." As evidence for what he called "the breadth and scope of new diplomatic departures," Alperovitz quoted Byrnes as having written that "those . . . days . . . were full of action.' "[37] In context, however, Byrnes was discussing merely the *number* of items which had to be dealt with at the war's end, including matters such as the visits of General Charles de Gaulle and Georges Bidault, new department appointments, and the like. He makes no mention of any "new diplomatic departures."[38]

Less obvious than his misuse of quotations, but no less insidious, is Alperovitz's habit of frequently altering in his own words what the sources actually say. Discussing American goals in Eastern Europe, he claimed that Byrnes "has written that both he and the President felt the attempt to reduce or eliminate Soviet influence in Southeastern Europe to be one of the most important objectives of American diplomacy at Potsdam."[39] In fact, Byrnes wrote that he and Truman wanted to reach agreements on four major issues, one of which was "plans for carrying out the Yalta Declaration on Liberated Europe, with the hope of ending the constant friction which had prevailed over Russian policy in eastern Europe since the Crimea Conference."[40] While the American interpreta-

[37] *Atomic Diplomacy*, 194. [38] *Speaking Frankly*, 92.

[39] *Atomic Diplomacy*, 146.

[40] *Speaking Frankly*, 67-68. Alperovitz rather consistently distorted what Byrnes had written. For example: "Byrnes has been quite explicit; his policy always aimed at forcing the Russians to yield in Eastern Europe, and in mid-1947 he still continued to argue that the United States had it in its power to force the Russians to 'retire in a very decent manner' " (*Atomic Diplomacy*,

tion of the Yalta agreements most certainly would have reduced Soviet influence in that area, the far more ambitious-sounding "or eliminate" is Alperovitz's construction purely and is not to be found in Byrnes's prose.

Finally, some statements in *Atomic Diplomacy* are directly refuted by the sources from which ostensibly they derive. In one such case, involving a meeting between Ambassador Harriman and Truman on April 20, 1945, Alperovitz has Harriman arguing that "a reconsideration of Roosevelt's policy was necessary."[41] Although Harriman did in fact argue for a reconsideration of earlier policy as manifested at Yalta (as he had during F.D.R.'s lifetime), Alperovitz neglected to add that the Ambassador believed Roosevelt already had reconsidered. By using the phrase "Roosevelt's policy" instead of "earlier policy," Alperovitz makes it appear that Harriman was trying to get Truman to abandon the position Roosevelt had taken by the time of his death. His reference, Truman's *Year of Decisions*, does not say this. It says, instead:

---

234). His source for this quotation is *Speaking Frankly*, 295. First of all, the phrase is Karl Marx's, taken from an article he wrote in 1853 having to do with Tsarist demands on Turkey. " 'If the other powers hold firm,' " Byrnes quoted Marx as having said, " 'Russia is sure to retire in a very decent manner.' " Byrnes cited Marx to show that Russian goals had not changed, and argued in his text that if the other powers in 1947 would "hold firm," Russia would not "violate the integrity of Iran, Turkey, Greece, Italy, or any other country." By weaving the quotation into his own prose in such a way as to make it appear that Byrnes referred to Poland, Bulgaria, Rumania, etc., Alperovitz completely altered the sense of what Byrnes actually wrote.

[41] *Atomic Diplomacy*, 22. The statement is repeated on 24.

Before leaving, Harriman took me aside and said, "Frankly, one of the reasons that made me rush back to Washington was the fear that you did not understand, as I had seen Roosevelt understand, that Stalin is breaking his agreements. My fear was inspired by the fact that you could not have had time to catch up with all the recent cables. But I must say that I am greatly relieved to discover that you have read them all and that we see eye to eye on the situation."[42]

Alperovitz's rendition of this discussion furthered his thesis that Truman broke with his predecessor's diplomacy, but did so at the expense of the facts.

Examples similar to the ones cited in this essay can be found throughout *Atomic Diplomacy*. They provide the foundations upon which its conclusions rest. That a trained scholar should have resorted to these practices in a book purporting to be a scholarly study is disconcerting. More disconcerting still is the fact that such a work could have come to be considered a contribution to the historical literature on the period.

[42] Truman, *Year of Decisions*, 72. Alperovitz's analysis of Harriman's activities emphasized the Ambassador's wish to move to a "showdown" over the Polish question. Yet, although he went into considerable detail (see 21-29) on the state of American–Russian relations concerning this issue, he omitted the fact that on April 1, less than two weeks before his death, Roosevelt had sent a strongly worded message to Stalin (undoubtedly one of the "recent cables" to which Harriman referred) telling him that the United States under no circumstances could accept the Soviet Union's interpretation of the Yalta accords as they applied to the formation of the Polish Provisional Government. Unless Truman retreated from this position, or Stalin from his, Roosevelt's cable made a showdown inevitable. A summary of this message can be found in Feis, *Churchill-Roosevelt-Stalin*, 575. Alperovitz mentioned Roosevelt's cable in an appendix (263-264), but minimized the adamant position Roosevelt had enunciated.

4.

THE FREE WORLD COLOSSUS: DAVID HOROWITZ

D AVID HOROWITZ's *The Free World Colossus: A Critique of American Foreign Policy in the Cold War* was all but ignored by professional historians when it first appeared in 1965. Despite this initial lack of interest in it, the book has become a standard work in the growing body of Cold War revisionism, and its republication in 1971 attests to its sustained popularity.[1] In his Preface to the new edition, Horowitz tried to account for the delayed recognition of his contribution. Until 1965, he wrote, "Cold War revisionism—that is, accounts of post-war history significantly at variance with the State Department line—was still illegitimate: it had no status as serious scholarship inside or outside the university." That year, however, as events in Southeast Asia began to "get out of hand" for the Lyndon B. Johnson Administration, "so the guardians of the academic establishment began to lose their control of the ivory tower." Revisionism, which began "finding an eager and receptive audience on the campuses," could be suppressed no longer.[2] The rest, one might say, is history. Nowhere did Horowitz even consider the possibility that charity rather than malice motivated those "guardians of the academic establish-

[1] Except where noted, the following critique is based upon the 1965 edition (New York: Hill & Wang).
[2] *Free World Colossus* (1971), 4-6.

ment" who snubbed his book, for the conscientious among them would have had to report that any resemblance *The Free World Colossus* bears to "serious scholarship" is at best superficial.

Horowitz's account of the Cold War's origins can best be described as a skeletonized version of D. F. Fleming's work without the latter's moderation.[8] Wartime relations between the United States and the Soviet Union, though strained at times, were fundamentally sound at the time of Franklin D. Roosevelt's death. With the accession of Harry S Truman the situation changed radically. Truman's natural belligerence and anti-Soviet attitudes, coupled with the emergence of militant advisors whom Roosevelt had restrained or ignored, spelled the end of collaboration. Almost immediately after his investiture, Truman moved to a crude "showdown" with the Soviet Union, following which he initiated a series of coercive acts designed to bring the Russians to heel. Stalin, bewildered at this sudden reversal, at first continued to seek accommodation with the United States. Then, as it became obvious that Truman meant to impinge upon areas Stalin deemed crucial to Russian national security, the Soviet position stiffened as well. The descent into Cold War, according to *The Free World Colossus*, came about largely as the result of unilateral American acts to which the Soviet Union reacted defensively.

In developing his themes, Horowitz left scarcely a canon of historical scholarship intact. He never used a primary document when a secondary or tertiary source

[8] In order to avoid repetition, I have tried in this essay to emphasize examples not previously discussed in the chapter on Fleming. Some duplication was unavoidable.

was available,[4] he repeatedly cited the unsupported assertions of others as though they constituted proof for his own assertions, and oftentimes he appeared to have confused his role as author with that of an editor. Compare, for instance, the following passages from Horowitz's book with excerpts from Howard K. Smith's journalistic *The State of Europe*, written in 1949:

The Free World Colossus (86-87)

Since 1942, America had displaced Britain as ruler of the seas, including "that most British of all waters," the east Mediterranean. By 1949, America was said to have a lien on some four hundred world-wide naval and air bases. This meant, "that any empire linked to its motherland by water exists on American sufferance, as it did last century on British sufferance—a fact that need never be expressed to have a profound influence on its policies." Pacts to standardize arms tied virtually the whole of North and South America to the United States. (The same arrangement was soon made with Western Europe.) This meant that it was nearly impossible for the attached nations either to enter or to stay out of war without the consent of the United States.

The State of Europe (70-71)

Since 1942 America had displaced Britain as ruler of the seas, including even that most British of all waters, the east Mediterranean. America is said to have a lien on some four hundred world-wide naval and air bases. This means that any empire linked to its motherland by water exists on American sufferance, as it did last century on British sufferance—a fact that need never be expressed to have a profound influence on its policies. . . . Pacts to standardize arms tie virtually the whole of North and South America to the United States. The same arrangement is being made with Western Europe . . . it means that it is nearly impossible for attached nations either to enter or to stay out of . . . war, without the consent of the supplying nation.

The Free World Colossus (89)

During the war, all three of the major allies had occupied Iran in order to assure wartime oil supplies to Russia; this seemed a prudent step in view of the Iranian Government's flirtation with the Nazis. After the war, it was agreed that all three should move out simultaneously,

The State of Europe (96-97)

All three great Allies had occupied . . . [Persia] to assure wartime supplies to Russia in face of the dubious attitude of the Persian government. After the war it was agreed that all three should move out simultaneously. But the Russians stayed on beyond their promised dead-

[4] Although Horowitz referred frequently to decisions reached at Yalta, for instance, he relied entirely on secondary sources rather than on the indispensable *Yalta Papers*, a volume in the *Foreign Relations of the United States* series. Nor did he use the *Potsdam Papers*, a similar collection of primary source materials.

but the Russians stayed beyond the deadline. During this time, they fomented a rebellion against the central Iranian Government in the Soviet-occupied areas of northern Iran and set up a friendly 'autonomous' government there. By this pressure they were able to induce the central government to grant them oil-exploitation rights in northern Iran. Russian aims were to win oil resources to supplement the production of their own badly damaged Caucasian fields.

The Western powers condemned these actions in the Security Council and, in May, the force of public opinion induced the Russians to withdraw from Iran. Then the central Iranian Government sent troops to break up the autonomous Azerbaijan Government. With this accomplished the Iranian parliament denounced the oil agreement with Russia.

line. They used the time to foment a rebellion against the central Persian Government in the Soviet-occupied areas of Northern Persia and to set up an "autonomous" regional government amicable to Russia there. . . . they induced the Persian central government to grant the oil-exploitation rights in northern Persia. The aims of the Russians were to win security against a country that had flirted with the Nazis during the war and to win oil resources to supplement those of the Soviets' badly damaged Caucasian fields. But their means to these ends were ugly.

The Western powers rightly condemned Russia's behavior in the Security Council, and the pressure of opinion eventually forced the Russians to withdraw from Persia. Then the Persian central government sent troops north and broke up the autonomous Azerbaijan government . . . and the Persian parliament denounced the oil agreement with Russia.

Except for expunging those of Smith's words which were critical of the Soviet Union, Horowitz reproduced these and other passages almost verbatim from *The State of Europe*. Occasionally he acknowledged that portions of his work were "based on" or "taken from" Smith's volume, which phrases constitute the only examples of understatement to be found in the book. These offenses are relatively trivial, however, when compared with the uses to which he put his materials.

Horowitz introduced his basic theme, that Truman reversed Roosevelt's policy of cooperation with the Soviet Union, in a vivid fashion. At the beginning of his first chapter he cited a message F.D.R. had sent, shortly before his death, to British Prime Minister Winston S.

Churchill: "I would minimize the general Soviet problem as much as possible because these problems, in one form or another, seem to arise every day, and most of them straighten out, as in the case of the Bern meeting.[5] We must be firm, however, and our course thus far is correct." These "measured and confident" words, Horowitz wrote, "serve as a logical starting point for a study of its [the wartime coalition's] deterioration and eventual collapse." As evidence of how quickly this process began, he counterposed to F.D.R.'s moderate stance Truman's famous confrontation with Soviet People's Minister for Foreign Affairs Vyacheslav M. Molotov on April 23, just eleven days after Roosevelt's death, during which Truman in harsh terms accused the Russians of failing to live up to the Yalta accords. The President's behavior at this meeting exhibited a "striking new emphasis," according to Horowitz, "one which seemed far removed from any attempt to 'minimize the general Soviet problem.' " "The episode," he added, "is all the more remarkable because Stalin had sent Molotov to the US for the founding conference of the UN 'to give some immediate assurance to the American people to indicate his desire

[5] The Bern meeting involved preliminary talks between U.S.– British military representatives and the German SS officer General Karl Wolff, who believed he could convince the German Commander-in-Chief in Italy, Field Marshal Albert Kesselring, to surrender his forces. Advised of these talks, the Russians wanted them suspended until Soviet officers could participate. When the Western Allies refused this request, Stalin charged that they were negotiating a separate peace which would permit German forces to be moved to the Eastern front. Roosevelt angrily denied this charge, and a heated exchange of cables followed. Nothing came of the talks.

to continue on a cooperative basis with this country' despite Roosevelt's death."[6]

Contrasting the Truman–Molotov meeting with Roosevelt's message is effective and on its face appears to testify to what Horowitz called a "sudden shift" in American policy. This is an illusion, however, created by omitting the context in which F.D.R. sent his cable, Soviet actions during the period, and the actual circumstances surrounding Molotov's trip to the United States. A markedly different picture emerges when these factors are taken into account.

Roosevelt's message to Churchill was written within the framework of the vexatious Polish question.[7] At Yalta the two Western leaders and Stalin had concluded an agreement providing for the creation of a provisional government for Poland, which thereafter would sponsor free elections as soon as it became feasible to hold them. The provisional government was to be formed by "reorganizing" the so-called Lublin Committee (a pro-Soviet group formed in 1944 behind Red Army lines and installed in power as the Russians advanced) on a broader democratic basis "with the inclusion of democratic leaders from Poland itself and from Poles abroad."[8] This agreement represented a compromise between Stalin's

[6] *Free World Colossus*, 31-32.

[7] See Byrnes, *Speaking Frankly*, 58-59. For the full text of these messages, see *Foreign Relations of the United States, 1945* (Washington: Government Printing Office, 1967) v, 209-210. Hereafter cited as *FRUS, 1945*, with appropriate volume number. Publications appearing after Horowitz completed his manuscript will not be used as a part of this critique, but will be cited for the purposes of information and verification.

[8] *Yalta Papers*, 973.

wish merely to "enlarge" the Lublin government and the Roosevelt–Churchill position advocating formation of an entirely new structure among the contending factions— the Lublin group, the Polish government-in-exile in London, and the Polish underground. Roosevelt realized the agreement was vague, as there was no precise formula specifying the extent to which the Lublin government would be altered, but thought it was the best he could get under the circumstances.[9]

Since Yalta virtually no progress had been made. The three-man committee established by the Great Powers to effectuate the agreement had become stymied over Russia's insistence that the Lublin group had the right of veto over which Poles could be invited for consultations concerning the makeup of the proposed provisional government. Both Churchill and Roosevelt refused to accept this claim, and after an exchange of cables between them, Roosevelt on April 1 had sent a strongly worded message to Stalin advising him that the United States could not consider the Lublin Poles to have any such right of veto, nor could it countenance a "thinly disguised continuance" of the Lublin group as the provisional government provided for at Yalta.[10] When Stalin showed no sign of retreating on the veto question in his reply, Churchill, who previously had told both Roosevelt and Stalin that if the stalemate were not ended he would feel obliged to report to the House of Commons that negotiations over Poland had broken down, cabled Roosevelt for his opinion on how he should handle the matter in an appearance

[9] Feis, *Churchill-Roosevelt-Stalin*, 528-529.
[10] A summary of this message can be found *ibid.*, 575; it is printed in full in *FRUS, 1945* v, 194-196.

before the Commons scheduled for the following week.[11]

It is against this background that Roosevelt's message must be understood. His reply to Churchill, beginning with the sentence "I would minimize the general Soviet problem . . . ," is his recommendation that Churchill refrain from making any drastic announcement at that time rather than an expression of the President's own feelings about the issue. And his concluding sentence—"We must be firm, however, and our course thus far is correct"—refers not to the general policy of trying to get along with the Soviet Union, as might be inferred when it is read in isolation, but to the adamant stand he had conveyed to Stalin on April 1. That F.D.R. would have retreated subsequently is possible, but using this message to indicate that his mood was conciliatory and optimistic during his last hours is unwarranted.

Horowitz's failure to mention Russian moves also contributed to the notion of Truman's "breaking" with his predecessor's policy. In the week before F.D.R.'s death, the State Department learned of two ominous developments. First, the Soviet Union in direct violation of existing zonal arrangements had turned over to the Lublin Poles captured German territories. Second, Russian authorities in Poland had arrested sixteen Polish underground leaders who had presented themselves under the impression that the Russians meant to negotiate with them.[12] Both these reports were confirmed after Roosevelt's death. Then, despite Washington's plea that the

[11] Byrnes, *Speaking Frankly*, 58; see also *FRUS, 1945* v, 192, 209.

[12] Feis, *Churchill-Roosevelt-Stalin*, 579-580; and see *FRUS, 1945* v, 198, 201.

action be postponed until discussions could be held with Molotov, the Soviet Union concluded a mutual assistance pact with Lublin, the official announcement of which arrived on the same day that the Russian minister landed in Washington.[13] All these steps served to confirm what Roosevelt had feared and, according to his April 1st message at least, was determined to prevent: Russian consolidation of Lublin's rule over Poland, "thinly disguised" or not.

Horowitz's omission of details surrounding Molotov's trip itself furthered his theme at the expense of historical accuracy. For the implication in his version is that Truman unexpectedly launched into a tirade over Poland at a time when the Russian was merely paying his respects to the departed Roosevelt. In the first place, both British and American policymakers (including Roosevelt) suspected that Stalin's initial refusal to send Molotov to San Francisco represented a form of blackmail on the Polish question: if the Western powers would not recognize Lublin and invite it to the Conference as the legitimate government of Poland, then Russia no longer would consider the United Nations important enough to send her first-line representative.[14] When, upon Roosevelt's death, Harriman asked Stalin to send Molotov as a gesture, it was with the full understanding that the Polish issue would be discussed both in Washington and in San Francisco.[15] Actually, Truman first met with Molotov for an

[13] Feis, *Churchill-Roosevelt-Stalin*, 577-78; *FRUS, 1945* v, 234.

[14] Feis, *Churchill-Roosevelt-Stalin*, 574; *FRUS, 1945* I, 156; *FRUS, 1945* v, 187.

[15] The statement Horowitz quoted beginning "to give some assurance to the American people . . ." is taken from a memo Harry

exchange of diplomatic amenities on the 22nd not the 23rd, as Horowitz claimed. The point is that Truman's outburst came at the end of several days of fruitless negotiations as an expression of frustration rather than at the beginning as an intrusion upon Molotov's attempt to convey Russia's condolences to the United States. That Truman resorted to "undiplomatic" language all observers agree, but the circumstances of this incident were not as Horowitz described them.

Truman's vocabulary excepted, where in the events discussed above does the "sudden shift" in American policy appear? The new President's charge that Russia was failing to carry out the Yalta accords by treating with Lublin as the legitimate government of Poland and by trying to engineer its invitation to the San Francisco Conference in no way deviated from Roosevelt's position at the time of his death. And, events would show, the Polish government Truman later (in July) recognized turned out to be no more than "a thinly disguised continuance" of the Lublin government.[16]

Horowitz's practice of omitting pertinent facts resulted in distortions of the most serious kind. Consider, for example, his version of the Soviet–American clash over the admittance of Argentina into the United Nations. During most of the San Francisco Conference, he wrote, "a cordial and cooperative atmosphere prevailed,"

Hopkins wrote after the event and not from Stalin's words, as Horowitz's text makes it appear. See Hopkins's memo, printed in Robert E. Sherwood, *Roosevelt and Hopkins: An Intimate History* (New York: Harper and Brothers, 1948), 883-884.

[16] *Potsdam Papers* I, 735; *FRUS, 1945* v, 393-436. The "free elections" were never held.

which was broken only when "Washington ordered the United States delegation to push through the admission of Argentina."[17] Since Roosevelt had said at Yalta that Argentina ought not to be included as one of the original members of the world organization (because of the fascist nature of her government and her failure to join the war), Horowitz presented this as another manifestation of the "sudden shift" in American policy and as proof that the United States rather than Russia failed to carry out the Yalta accords in good faith. To corroborate this interpretation, he quoted Cordell Hull's remark that "irreparable harm had been done" by the vote to admit Argentina and that "if the American delegation were not careful we should get Russia into such a state of mind that she might decide that the United Nations organization was not going to furnish adequate security to her in the future." Hull, obviously identified with Rooseveltian policies, is made to appear as though he were protesting against Truman's "new" approach towards Russia.[18]

To begin with—and this is made plain in the sources used in *The Free World Colossus*—Truman *opposed* Argentina's admission and reversed himself only reluctantly.[19] At Yalta F.D.R. had agreed to sponsor the admission of the Ukraine and White Russia to the United

[17] *Free World Colossus*, 38.

[18] *Ibid.*, 39. The quotation is from Hull's *The Memoirs of Cordell Hull* (2 vols., New York: Macmillan, 1948) II, 1722.

[19] Arthur H. Vandenberg, Jr. (ed.), *The Private Papers of Senator Vandenberg* (Boston: Houghton Mifflin, 1952), 178; Sherwood, *Roosevelt and Hopkins*, 897-898. See also *FRUS, 1945* I, 411. Secretary of State Edward R. Stettinius, Jr., reported to the American delegation on April 25 that Truman was "dead set against Argentina's being admitted to the United Nations."

Nations, thereby giving the Soviet Union three votes in that organization. In trying to line up support for these admissions at San Francisco, however, the American delegation learned that the Latin American republics would cooperate only if Argentina got in as well.[20] Whether Roosevelt would have paid this price cannot be known, but Truman did so under the impression it was necessary to fulfill the pledges made at Yalta, not to violate them. Nor did Hull believe otherwise. Horowitz correctly cited Hull's statement about the impact this defeat (Russia tried unsuccessfully to tie Lublin's admission to Argentina's) might have on Russia's attitude, but he neglected to mention that the former Secretary of State well knew that the initiative had *not* come from Washington. Hull's complaint, in fact, was that "other delegations had outmaneuvered the United States on the Argentina question."[21]

Perhaps the most egregious use of this technique occurs in Horowitz's references to Senator Arthur H. Vandenberg of Michigan, who was one of the American delegates to the San Francisco Conference. By labeling Vandenberg "Truman's delegate" and identifying him as a man who by the time of the conference "had already become a key figure in shaping United States foreign policy," Horowitz portrayed Vandenberg, an avowed hardliner towards the Russians, as an accurate reflector of Truman's position.[22] Several lengthy excerpts from Van-

[20] Vandenberg, *Private Papers,* 177-178.

[21] Hull, *Memoirs* II, 1722.

[22] *Free World Colossus*, 37. As "proof" of Vandenberg's "key" role, Horowitz cited in a footnote the Senator's connection with the Marshall Plan, a program initiated several years after the period in question.

denberg's published *Private Papers* were cited as though they provided insights into Truman's thinking.[23] But what Horowitz failed to make clear is that F.D.R., not Truman, appointed Vandenberg and that at the time (as is plainly shown in the *Private Papers*) the Senator was not even privy to administration decisions, let alone responsible as a "key" figure for shaping them. Actually, Vandenberg on several occasions expressed doubts about Truman's willingness to stand up to the Russians as he would have liked.[24]

Truman's motives and actions invariably are presented in *The Free World Colossus* in a manner designed to emphasize his culpability for deteriorating relations with the Soviet Union. When mere omissions proved insufficient, Horowitz often fell back upon what might be termed "history by insinuation." Harry Hopkins's mission to Moscow in the late Spring of 1945 provides a good example. Truman's decision to send Hopkins to seek a way out of the Polish impasse posed a problem to Horowitz, as it has for most revisionists. If the new President already had decided to abandon his predecessor's diplomacy, why send to represent him in talks with Stalin a man so closely identified with Rooseveltian policies? Without saying so directly, Horowitz implied that Tru-

[23] *Ibid.*, 37, 38, 50-51.
[24] See Vandenberg, *Private Papers*, Chapters II and III. On May 9 Vandenberg complained in his diary "there is no longer any strong hand on our foreign policy" (191); on May 20 he wrote that he did "not doubt for an instant" that Roosevelt, had he lived, "would force a showdown with Stalin" over the Yalta pledges (197); and on June 8 he alleged that "we had an indication from Washington . . . that the 'appeasement' spirit was similarly seeping into the White House" (209).

man's move actually was a ruse devised to glean from
an unwitting Stalin concessions which the Russian leader
thought would insure the continuity of wartime collaboration at a time when the administration already had
concluded that such collaboration would not continue.
As not a shred of evidence has yet emerged to support
this allegation, Horowitz resorted to indirection. Thus:

> There was an element of cynicism, unconscious perhaps,
> in the decision to send Harry Hopkins, already a "seri-
> ously ill" man, to parley with Stalin. Hopkins himself
> was surprised when Truman agreed to the suggestion
> that he undertake the mission, for Hopkins had been the
> key man in implementing Roosevelt's approach to the
> Soviet Union, an approach that had already fallen into
> disrepute.[25]

While the "unconscious perhaps" waffled on the charge
of cynicism, Horowitz's statement that Truman's decision
surprised Hopkins for the reason indicated is without
foundation in fact. Neither Robert E. Sherwood's *Roosevelt and Hopkins*, upon which Horowitz based his analysis
of this episode, nor any other source used in *The Free
World Colossus* even so much as suggests this was so or
that Hopkins believed he stood for "an approach that
had already fallen into disrepute."[26]

Throughout his account of the mission, to which he
devoted an entire chapter, Horowitz used similar methods to convey the impression that Truman acted hypo-
critically. Ambassador Harriman, who accompanied
Hopkins during his talks with Stalin, served as Horowitz's vehicle. As Harriman even before Roosevelt's

[25] *Free World Colossus*, 42.
[26] Sherwood, *Roosevelt and Hopkins*, 883, 887.

death had been urging that the United States adopt a firmer approach toward the Soviet Union, Horowitz portrayed him as a symbol of the "new" diplomacy and hinted that he was "in" on the scheme of which Hopkins was unaware. The very fact that Harriman had expressed enthusiasm over the Hopkins's mission, for instance, Horowitz found "disconcerting."[27] And, discussing Hopkins's effort to convince Stalin that the manner in which Lend-Lease aid had been curtailed in early May did not constitute an effort to coerce the Soviet Union, Horowitz resorted to the rhetorical "one can only wonder what Ambassador Harriman thought as he listened to this plea. . . . For Harriman had been the most persistent spokesman for the position that precisely this kind of pressure tactic *must* be used against the Soviet Union in order to compel the Russians to cooperate."[28] Although he adduced no evidence to show either that the curtailment was intended as a coercive act or that Harriman had urged it as such, Horowitz parlayed these allegations into "evidence" that Hopkins was being used by a cynical ("unconscious perhaps") administration.[29]

[27] *Free World Colossus*, 46.

[28] *Ibid.*, 43-44 (Horowitz's emphasis).

[29] Horowitz attempted to substantiate his charge about Harriman as follows: "He had, in fact, called for the selection of 'one or two cases' where Soviet actions had been 'intolerable' and urged 'effective reprisals' in order to make the Soviets realize that they 'cannot continue their present attitude except at great cost to themselves'" (44). But the phrase "effective reprisals" is not Harriman's, as Horowitz made it appear, but Walter Millis's, and it can be found on page 40 of *The Forrestal Diaries*, which Millis with the collaboration of E. S. Duffield edited. It is true that Harriman had been calling for a firmer policy towards the Soviet Union, but no evidence has yet been adduced to show that he

In his presentation of the negotiations between Hopkins and Stalin, Horowitz moved from omission and insinuation into inexcusable misconstructions of the historical record. Three examples will suffice. Referring to Hopkins's opening remarks to Stalin, Horowitz wrote that Hopkins "was not able to offer concretely the goodwill of the American leadership, but only that of American public opinion," thereby making it seem as though Hopkins's instructions did not include any expression of desire on the administration's part to cooperate with the Soviet Union.[30] But his source, Charles E. Bohlen's notes of the conversations, printed in Sherwood's *Roosevelt and Hopkins*, flatly contradicts this assertion.

> Prior to his departure [Hopkins said] President Truman had expressed to him his great anxiety at the present situation and also his desire to continue President Roosevelt's policy of working with the Soviet Union and his intention to carry out in fact as well as in spirit all the arrangements, both formal and informal, which President Roosevelt and Marshal Stalin had worked out together.[31]

One might argue that Truman was insincere, but that is another matter; Horowitz's allegation is simply untrue.

Seeking to contrast Stalin's "amicability" with American militance, Horowitz also misrepresented the manner in which certain decisions were reached.[32] While Hopkins

---

did in fact recommend the Lend-Lease curtailment as it was effected by subordinate officials.

[30] *Free World Colossus*, 47.
[31] *Roosevelt and Hopkins*, 889.
[32] *Free World Colossus*, 49.

was in Moscow, for instance, a dispute arose in San Francisco over the veto question. On June 1 the Russian delegate, Andrei Gromyko, announced that Russia's position on the veto power of permanent members of the Security Council was that this power should extend even to the matter of determining subjects to be discussed by the Council. Hopkins was advised to take up the issue with Stalin and to tell him that under no circumstances could the United States accept such a broad interpretation of the veto power. Horowitz, after quoting passages from Hopkins's appeal for a modification of Russia's new stance, concluded as follows:

> At this point, Molotov entered the discussion to defend the Soviet position, but Stalin cut him off. Then "Marshal Stalin . . . stated that he had no objection to a simple majority being applied in discussions relating to pacific settlement." The veto crisis was over.[33]

The record tells a different story. Horowitz's "Stalin cut him off" conceals the import of the following passage from Bohlen's notes:

> (Ensued a conversation in Russian [which Bohlen spoke fluently] between Mr. Molotov and Marshal Stalin from which it was clear that the Marshal had not understood the issues involved and had not had them explained to him. During this conversation Marshal Stalin remarked that he thought it was an insignificant matter and that they should accept the American position.)[34]

Thus, what Horowitz termed an "important concession" actually occurred over an issue about which Stalin had

[33] *Ibid.*, 50.
[34] Sherwood, *Roosevelt and Hopkins*, 911.

been uninformed until that time and which, in any event, he thought "insignificant."

A final instance of such methods can be seen in Horowitz's account of Harriman's report on the talks. Citing the Ambassador's views, as related by Truman in his *Year of Decisions*, that Stalin "*took the offensive* in complaining 'about our misdeeds' and *aggressively* indicated that if we did not wish to deal on a friendly basis with the Soviet Union, she was strong enough to look after herself," Horowitz wrote: "In the public record of the Stalin–Hopkins talks, the only remark by Stalin which can be bent into this mold was that quoted in regard to Lend-Lease Aid."[35] And that remark, in *The Free World Colossus*, is presented as "quite clearly an attempt to help Hopkins out of an embarrassing position . . . ."[36]

Once again, the "record" refutes Horowitz's words. Stalin opened the second meeting (the first was given over to reminiscences, exchanges concerning what subjects would be discussed, etc.) by alluding to "recent moves" by the United States Government which, he said, had caused "a certain alarm" within Soviet circles. He mentioned five such moves and included in his elucidation of them the phrases "brutal," "had raised the question of the value of agreements between the three major

---

[35] *Free World Colossus*, 51 (Horowitz's emphasis). Truman's statement is taken from his *Year of Decisions*, 262. Horowitz misplaced the quotation marks in reproducing this passage, which reads: "He took the offensive in complaining 'about our misdeeds and aggressively indicated that if we did not wish to deal on a friendly basis with the Soviet Union, she was strong enough to look after herself.' "

[36] *Free World Colossus*, 51.

powers," "an insult to the Soviet Union," "an attempt to humiliate the Russians," and "the Russians should not be regarded as fools." He said, furthermore, that "much could be done" between the United States and Russia if the Soviet Union were approached on a friendly basis, but that reprisals in any form would "bring about the opposite effect."[37] Horowitz, rather than Harriman, misrepresented Stalin's behavior.

Horowitz closed his chapter on Hopkins's mission with a quotation from a memorandum Hopkins wrote six months after the Moscow talks:

> *"Our Russian policy must not be dictated by people who have already made up their minds there is no possibility of working with the Russians and that our interests are bound to conflict and ultimately lead to war. From my point of view, this is an untenable position and can but lead to disaster."*

This "perceptive" and "prophetic" comment, according to Horowitz, represented Hopkins's opinion "on the change that had taken place in the United States approach to the Soviet Union."[38] It was nothing of the sort. In context, Hopkins was not referring to the Truman administration at all, but to "a small, vociferous minority" of Americans, of whom he said: "They represent nobody but themselves and no government worth its salt in control of our country would ever permit that group to influence our official actions." There is nothing in this memorandum that so much as hints at any "change" in

[37] Sherwood, *Roosevelt and Hopkins*, 893-895.
[38] *Free World Colossus*, 52 (Horowitz's emphasis).

policy between Roosevelt and Truman, nor is there any criticism of the latter's conduct.[39] Horowitz's version of what Hopkins wrote is a pure fabrication.

Instances of citing an individual's words from one context in order to "prove" something in another clot the pages of *The Free World Colossus*. Few escape. Horowitz's evaluation of Truman's attitude towards the Yalta Conference is typical. Citing the President's comment that "our agreements with the Soviet Union so far have been a one-way street and that he could not continue," Horowitz presented this as evidence that Truman thought the decisions reached at Yalta were "simply allied concessions to Russian demands." "The historical record provides no support" for such an estimate, he concluded, and quoted Edward R. Stettinius's later statement that "the Soviet Union made more concessions to the United States and Great Britain than were made to the Soviet Union. . . ."[40] What the historical record actually shows is that Truman directed his remark at what he believed were Russian violations of the Yalta accords, not at the accords as such.[41]

W. Averell Harriman, who prowls the pages of *The Free World Colossus* as a grey eminence constantly goading the administration into ever more belligerent postures, incurs the same treatment numerous times. The most flagrant example can be found in Horowitz's discussion of a meeting held among administration officials shortly before Truman met with Molotov on April 23.

[39] The entire memorandum is in Sherwood's *Roosevelt and Hopkins*, 921-925. The quotation is from 923.

[40] *Free World Colossus*, 35.

[41] Millis, *Forrestal Diaries*, 50.

Concerning Secretary of War Henry L. Stimson's contention that Russia thus far had lived up to her larger military commitments, Horowitz quoted Harriman's reply that these " 'were decisions the U.S.S.R. had already reached by itself, *but on other military matters it was impossible to say that they had lived up to their commitments. For example, over a year ago they had agreed to start on preparations for collaboration in the Far Eastern war, but none of these had been carried out.*' " After alluding to America's failure to open a second front in Europe by 1942, Horowitz went on to say that subsequent events "served, dramatically, to expose the emptiness" of Harriman's judgement. Since at Yalta Stalin had promised to enter the Far Eastern war three months after the defeat of Germany, and since Russia *had* declared war "three months to the day" after Germany's surrender, "precisely that portion of the Yalta agreement which Harriman seized upon as evidence that the Russians were not keeping their agreements was fulfilled by them *to the letter.*"[42]

Horowitz's exposure of Harriman's "error" is fatuous for the simple reason that Harriman's comment had nothing to do either with Yalta or with the date of Russia's entry into the war. His reference to agreements made "over a year ago" makes this plain at the most cursory reading, inasmuch as the Yalta Conference had ended less than three months before. What Harriman was talking about were arrangements he had made with Stalin for the construction of strategic air force bases and other installations in eastern Russia. Those agreements had been made "over a year ago," and Harriman found sub-

[42] *Free World Colossus*, 44-46 (Horowitz's emphasis).

sequently that the Russians refused to move ahead on them.[43] His comment was perfectly appropriate, therefore, when applied to the right subject.

James F. Byrnes, who succeeded Stettinius as Secretary of State, fared just as badly in *The Free World Colossus.* On the question of Soviet entry into the war against Japan, one finds:

> On July 29, Molotov called [Byrnes] again and said that Stalin had instructed him to discuss (with Truman and Byrnes) "the immediate cause of the Soviet Union's entry into the war." "The request," wrote Byrnes later, "presented a problem to us." "The Soviet Union," Byrnes explained, "had a non-aggression pact with the Japanese. . . . We did not believe that the United States Government should be placed in the position of asking another government to violate its agreement without good and sufficient reason. . . . The President was disturbed."

Thus, Horowitz makes it appear that Truman and Byrnes, who he alleged were at this time trying to prevent Russia from entering the war, sought to avoid even discussing the matter by resorting to legalisms. Such "intense concern for the niceties of international law," he concluded, in a stunning *non sequitur*, "seems scarcely credible in view of the administration's willingness to atomize the 400,000 inhabitants of Hiroshima and Nagasaki at a moment when their government was suing for peace."[44]

In reality, the "request" Byrnes spoke of was not Stalin's wish to discuss the issue; it was the latter's proposal that the United States, Great Britain, and the other

[43] See Deane, *The Strange Alliance*, 229-235.
[44] *Free World Colossus*, 57.

allies should "address a formal request to the Soviet Government for its entry into the war." This is what "presented a problem" and "disturbed" Truman, for acceding to it would place the United States in the position of publicly and formally asking the Soviet Union to violate its treaty with Japan. Instead, Byrnes wrote a memorandum (which Truman signed) to Stalin suggesting that the Soviet Union enter the war on the grounds of the Moscow Declaration of October 30, 1943, and several provisions of the United Nations Charter.[45] Whatever Truman and Byrnes thought about Russia privately, they made no effort to deter her entrance. Horowitz, in the manner of the late Al Smith, repeatedly called for a look at the "record" but rarely got straight what the record actually says.

"By an examination of the fictional basis of Western, cold war mythology," Horowitz announced in his Preface, "it is the hope of this essay to lay the foundations for a more accurate understanding of the U. S. role during the cold war decades."[46] Surely this is an admirable goal, but one that is difficult to reach by the methods detailed in the preceding pages. Far from being a piece of "serious" scholarship—or scholarship of any kind—*The Free World Colossus* is little more than a polemic with footnotes.

[45] Byrnes, *Speaking Frankly*, 207-209.
[46] *Free World Colossus*, 15.

5.

THE POLITICS OF WAR:
GABRIEL KOLKO

IN recent years a growing number of revisionist historians have devoted their attention to World War II as well as its immediate aftermath. Of the works thus far produced, Gabriel Kolko's *The Politics of War: The World and United States Foreign Policy, 1943-1945* is the most comprehensive.[1] Scholars of all persuasions greeted this book as a formidable assault on "orthodox" interpretations. Phrases such as "immense achievement," "the most important and stimulating discussion of American policy during World War II to appear in more than a decade," "provocative, intrepid," and "a turning point in the historiography of the war and postwar period" are some of the more effusive pronouncements reviewers bestowed upon *The Politics of War*.[2] What apparently has escaped notice, however, is that the book also contains an enormous number of factual errors and its interpretations frequently rest upon insupportable renditions of documentary materials.

Stated briefly, Kolko's thesis is that American foreign

[1] (New York: Random House, 1968.)

[2] The phrases cited above are taken from the following reviews, listed in order: Ronald Radosh, *Nation* 209 (October 6, 1969), 350-351; Gaddis Smith, *New York Times Book Review* (April 13, 1969), 6; Thomas G. Paterson, *Journal of American History* LVI (December 1969), 712-714; Hans J. Morgenthau, *New York Review of Books* 13 (July 10, 1969), 10-17.

policy during World War II had as its consuming goal the creation of a postwar economic order the purpose of which would be to further American expansion and penetration throughout the world. This new order—"an integrated world capitalism," to use his term—necessarily required the establishment of political systems amenable to American ambitions. Assuming the defeat of Germany and Japan, American policymakers during the course of the war came to define as major obstacles to success the Soviet Union, the emerging Left in Europe and Asia (which Americans consistently, and wrongly, thought to be Moscow-dominated), and Great Britain's efforts to retain as much as possible of her pre-war imperial system. Although disagreeing frequently over specific policies, American officials pursued their broad economic ends with a single-minded ardor and in the process never hesitated to break agreements, betray allies, or sell out the freedoms of smaller countries. By repeatedly colliding with the Soviet Union (which was merely trying to attain its legitimate security needs), moreover, the United States bore the major responsibility for the onset of the Cold War.

Many elements of Kolko's story are familiar, despite his somewhat breathless presentations. General American antipathy toward the Left, the questionable "deals" made with French and Italian Rightists, and Stalin's pragmatic relations with non-Russian Communists, to name a few, are subjects to which Kolko adds little. Nor is his overall thesis original, having been advanced years earlier by, among others, William Appleman Williams.[3]

[3] See especially his *The Tragedy of American Diplomacy*, rev. edn., Chapter VI.

What is impressive about *The Politics of War* is its force-
ful prose, its author's ability to weave into his theoretical
framework issues relating to almost every aspect of the
war, and the apparent thoroughness with which he documented his interpretations. One must say "apparent," for
when the sources themselves are consulted, discrepancies
of the most appalling magnitude appear.

A comprehensive examination of Kolko's book, which
runs to almost 700 pages, is impossible to present in the
space of an essay. Some idea of his methods can be conveyed, however, by examples taken from his prominent
themes—relations with Great Britain, the Left, and the
Soviet Union—and from his handling of the war's military aspects. This latter subject often is crucial to Kolko's
interpretations of Washington's policies toward its wartime allies, for apparent deviations from his basic thesis
are seen as mere expediencies dictated by the fortunes of
war, to be rectified at more propitious times.

Kolko's account of the latter part of the war in Europe
is characteristic. By late Fall of 1944, he wrote, the Western Allies had bogged down owing to "caution" and "a
critical gasoline shortage at least partially the result of
the vast black-market operations of American soldiers."
The British, who did not suffer such shortages, could not
carry the load alone. Then, in December, "despite overwhelming American and British superiority in arms and
men," the Germans launched an attack in the Ardennes
forest that "routed" Anglo-American armies and threatened large parts of Belgium. Responding to General
Dwight D. Eisenhower's frantic pleas, Roosevelt and
Churchill importuned Stalin to come to the aid of their
beleaguered forces. The Russian leader generously con-

105

sented and, "despite poor weather and incomplete preparations," mounted a winter offensive ahead of schedule, thereby forcing the Germans to withdraw from the Ardennes to meet "the Russian hordes." By the time of the Yalta Conference (February 4-11), Roosevelt and Churchill represented forces that were "failing" and had to treat with Russia accordingly. When the Anglo-American armies subsequently did resume offensive operations, it was because the "flood" of German troops moving from west to east permitted them to advance virtually unopposed.[4]

In his zeal to underscore the enormity and success of the Soviet Union's offensive as contrasted with America's puny efforts in the West, Kolko lingered over casualties the Russians inflicted, prisoners taken, and divisions smashed.[5] Those figures he provided for the western front tend to show what an easy time Anglo-American forces had: for instance, that American armies crossed the Rhine "with the loss of fourteen men."[6] On the whole, Kolko gave the distinct impression that America's part in the closing months of the war in Europe consisted of selling gasoline on the black market, breaking under attack, and moving forward only when confronted by skeleton forces. No battles other than the Ardennes were mentioned, and American air operations went ignored.

Kolko's presentation is wildly inaccurate on every level. What he neglected to point out was that German troops were shifting from east to west in the latter months of 1944, and that Hitler denied the eastern front much-

[4] *Politics of War*, 350-353, 370-372.
[5] *Ibid.*, 352, 372.   [6] *Ibid.*, 372.

needed reinforcements and equipment in order to mount the Ardennes assault.[7] Anglo-American forces stopped that attack, furthermore, two weeks *before* the Russian offensive began.[8] One need not minimize Russia's enormous sacrifices throughout the war to say that events in the west during the winter of 1944-1945 helped to insure Soviet successes rather than the other way around. And Anglo-American armies were not "failing" by the time of Yalta; they already were engaged in limited offensives in preparation for closing to the Rhine.[9]

Kolko's passages describing these months are freighted with quotations and heavily documented, but he got very nearly all his facts wrong. Gasoline shortages occurred because American and British armies had pushed much farther inland than the planners had anticipated, and British fuel supplies depended upon allocations decided by Eisenhower rather than upon the innate honesty of the British soldier.[10] Allied armies in the west did not have an "overwhelming superiority in arms and men" in December 1944, most certainly not in the Ardennes.[11] Eisenhower did not ask about the Russian offensive because he thought it might come in time to stop the German attack; he wanted to know for the purpose of plan-

[7] Chester Wilmot, *The Struggle for Europe* (New York: Harper and Brothers, 1952), 621-622. Working from German records, Wilmot estimated that at least seventeen divisions moved from the eastern to the western front during the last six months of 1944. The preponderance of aircraft, armor, and artillery was allocated to the western front in this period.

[8] Forrest C. Pogue, *The Supreme Command* (Washington: Department of the Army, 1954), 407.

[9] *Ibid.*, 417-419.

[10] *Ibid.*, 251, 256-259, 284, 292.

[11] Wilmot, *Struggle*, 580-582.

ning future operations whether he could depend upon the Russians to halt or reverse the flow of German troops.[12]

Even in carrying out the elementary task of copying down correctly the figures listed in his sources, Kolko got almost everything wrong. All of his "mistakes," moreover, served to confirm his thesis. The subject of German troop concentrations, which Kolko makes much of to show the relative contributions of Russia and the Western Allies, provides such an instance. At Yalta, he wrote, the Russians reported that sixteen German divisions had shifted from the western to the eastern front, that five were in transition, and that thirty to thirty-five more would be moved in the near future.[13] Thus, according to Kolko, out of approximately eighty German divisions on the western front at the beginning of 1945, more than fifty moved east, leaving to fight the Anglo-American armies by late March only twenty-six divisions, and "most of this small number held the northern German ports . . . ."[14] His figures add up correctly, give or take a division or two, and, together with his failure to count in German forces on the Italian front, emphasize dramatically his contention that American troops engaged only a tiny portion of the German army.[15] They are, however, false.

The Russian estimates of German movements that Kolko cited can be found in the *Yalta Papers*.[16] But, as the document makes clear, Soviet military authorities

---

[12] Stephen E. Ambrose, *The Supreme Commander: The War Years of General Dwight D. Eisenhower* (New York: Doubleday, 1970), 599-600.

[13] *Politics of War*, 352.   [14] *Ibid.*, 372.

[15] There were approximately twenty-seven German divisions on the Italian front. See *Yalta Papers*, 577.

[16] *Ibid.*, 583.

never believed that all reinforcements for the east had been, or would be, taken away from the western front. Of the sixteen divisions that had already arrived, for instance, only six came from the western front; the rest were from Italy, the German interior, and other parts of Europe. The figure of thirty to thirty-five divisions, from the same document, is the number that the Russians thought Germany *might* move eastward unless the United States and Great Britain resumed offensive operations and mounted intensive air attacks. This estimate, in *The Politics of War*, is transmuted into actual troop movements. Finally, the figure of twenty-six divisions remaining in the west as of late March seems to have been taken from Forrest C. Pogue's *The Supreme Command*. But Pogue did not write that there were only twenty-six divisions left in the west; rather, he said that because Anglo-American armies had so badly mauled the Germans during the winter and early spring that the "more than sixty" divisions existing on paper had a combat effectiveness of only twenty-six fully manned units.[17] Thus Kolko's account of German troop deployments is almost pure fiction.

It would be worth calling attention to Kolko's version of military events if only to illustrate the biases which permeate his book. But he used it to undergird nearly every aspect of his analysis of the Yalta Conference as well as a number of other episodes which took place during the last months of the war in Europe. Stalin's refusal at Yalta to exploit the military situation, for instance, to Kolko showed that the Russian "was prepared naively to grant more to Western interests than he asked in return."

[17] Pogue, *Supreme Command*, 427.

Churchill and Roosevelt reacted far less honorably. Aware that their forces were "failing," they deliberately sought vague agreements which later they could interpret to their own satisfaction. "Quite intentionally," Kolko wrote, "in the hope that subsequent power balances would be more favorable, the United States and Britain left the final accords subject to much further clarification and agreement, an obscurity that could lead to immediate agreement and subsequent dispute."[18]

Although those pages in *The Politics of War* dealing with military affairs probably contain the highest ratio of distortions per paragraph, Kolko's treatment of wartime relations with Yugoslavia scores nearly as high. In keeping with his theme of Washington's unrelenting fear and hatred of the Left, Kolko repeatedly stated that the United States nourished the forces of Draza Mihailovic, whom the State Department knew to be collaborating with the enemy, while at the same time denying aid to Tito's more popular Partisan army.[19] To sustain this latter point, Kolko at one place has American officials investigating "rumors that American arms were being sent to Tito in violation of standing orders" and cited a State Department memo to the effect " 'that we disapprove of any plan for building up the Tito forces at the expense of the Serbs. . . .' "[20]

Again, Kolko's allegations are wrong almost without exception, which feat he managed by ignoring some documents and misrepresenting others. Whatever the truth of Mihailovic's "full collaboration with the Axis," Kolko's statement that "virtually all admitted" it at the time is

[18] *Politics of War*, 368.   [19] *Ibid.*, 131-138.
[20] *Ibid.*, 134.

incorrect. Reports coming into the State Department denied this charge, as did briefing papers made up within the department.[21] More important, the United States *did* furnish weapons and supplies to Tito, contrary to what Kolko wrote, and on one occasion (in cooperation with the British) carried out a series of air strikes against German forces which had surrounded Tito and his men. Tito's letter to Roosevelt "expressing my gratitude to you for the assistance in material and in the cooperation of your Air Force," published in the *Foreign Relations* series (from which, on other matters, Kolko quoted exhaustively), may have struck the author of *The Politics of War* as being unsuited to his needs.[22] And the State Department memo that Kolko offered as evidence of American leaders' opposition to giving aid to Tito actually was written within the context of a rumored attack by the Partisans against Mihailovic's Chetniks. The quoted passage, hence, refers to arms for use against other Yugoslavians, not Germans.[23]

In providing another illustration of American attitudes toward the Left, Kolko garbled what the documents say about the situation in Greece. There, he claimed, even though American officials knew full well of widespread Royalist atrocities against Leftist factions, they unhesi-

[21] *FRUS, 1944* IV, 1336, 1351, 1366, 1387. Some Americans claimed that Mihailovic seemed more interested in jockeying for position against Tito than in fighting Germans, but generally they dismissed rumors of collaboration as British propaganda.

[22] Ambrose, *Eisenhower*, 305; Feis, *Churchill-Roosevelt-Stalin*, 354. Tito's letter is in *FRUS, 1944* IV, 1356-1357.

[23] *FRUS, 1944* IV, 1398-1399. Kolko merely omitted the latter part of the sentence, which reads: "and naturally we are disturbed by the reports that American arms are being supplied to Tito for use in this civil war."

tatingly backed British efforts to prop up the Royalist government. At Potsdam, according to Kolko, the Americans had in their possession "a detailed report, carefully prepared" by the staff of the American Ambassador in Greece, fully describing what Kolko referred to as the greatest example of "naked repression and nationalist jingoism in all Europe." It was "in this factual context," he wrote, that "the Big Three debated the subject of Greece at Potsdam."[24]

Kolko wholly misrepresented the contents of the report, which directly contradicts his allegations. As the Ambassador himself said in a covering letter, the information it contained "fails to support in any substantial degree the allegations of Marshal Tito and the Moscow and Balkan Soviet press regarding anarchy and wholesale terror in Northern Greece."[25] Within the report terms such as "flight of fancy" are used to describe Tito's charges. The document's substance is that the "Greek Government authorities seem to be following a middle-of-the-road course and sinning more by omission than by commission."[26]

Kolko's use of the document itself is illuminating. The report, he said, "admitted 'the deficiencies of present Greek regional administrative and judicial procedure . . . for the civil liberties of leftists and Slavophones [Macedonians].' "[27] His ellipses replaced the middle of the quotation: "and the disregard of local officials of royalist persuasion."[28] Thus, a statement that the Greek government was inefficient and that certain local officials were

[24] *Politics of War*, 584.
[26] *Ibid.*, 1051, 1055.
[28] *Potsdam Papers* II, 1049.

[25] *Potsdam Papers* II, 1049.
[27] *Politics of War*, 584.

repressing Leftist factions becomes "proof" of something rather different. Later in the same paragraph, referring to Greek-Albanian border incidents, Kolko has the American embassy in Albania attributing "most of the difficulty of that region to British officers and 'the Greeks who started propaganda campaign on frontier problems and persecution.' "[29] This, too, is false. "I cannot say positively which side is stirring up these border incidents," the Ambassador wrote, even though he admitted his "opinion is colored by Albanian point of view because it was the Greeks who started propaganda campaign on frontier problems and persecution."[30] He expressed equal uncertainty about British complicity.

The treatment of American relations with Great Britain found in *The Politics of War* is no less misleading. As evidence for his theme of almost constant friction between the two nations, for instance, Kolko repeated the old tale of Winston Churchill's shock and disagreement over the policy of "unconditional surrender" Roosevelt unveiled at Casablanca.[31] Since this particular myth was dispelled more than fifteen years ago, and since Kolko included in his covering footnote one of the books which helped dispel it, one can only wonder whether he read his source or simply disregarded it.[32]

[29] *Politics of War*, 584.   [30] *Potsdam Papers* II, 1063.
[31] *Politics of War*, 24.
[32] See John L. Chase, "Unconditional Surrender Reconsidered," *Political Science Quarterly* LXX (June 1955), 258-279. This is reprinted in Robert A. Divine (ed.), *Causes and Consequences of World War II* (Chicago: Quadrangle, 1969), 183-201. Kolko's footnote refers to Feis, *Churchill-Roosevelt-Stalin*, 108-110. As Chase and Feis make clear, Churchill may have been surprised by F.D.R.'s timing, but not by the policy itself. Nor did

113

If his account of the "unconditional surrender" issue can be attributed to an oversight, his handling of other matters makes such an explanation less convincing. Consider the following passage:

> For the rest of 1944 State Department advisers urged pinning the British down, and showed less and less sympathy for their economic plight as the British hesitated. Everywhere, from the Middle East and Latin America to direct conferences, any discussion of foreign economic policy with the British moved from bad to worse. "The combination of all these things," John D. Hickerson, the department's chief expert on Britain, warned in November, "may bring about an uproar which will result in a situation that will make U.S.–U.K. relations after World War I (and God knows they were bad then) look like a love feast by comparison."[33]

Actually, Hickerson's comments appear in a report which squarely refutes Kolko's thesis about what State Department advisors were urging. It was in America's interests, Hickerson wrote, "short term and long term, to have a post-war Britain that is as strong as she can be made," and he discussed as one tool "Phase II" of Lend Lease,

---

he disagree with it at that time, as indicated by his message to the War Cabinet several days earlier: "We propose to draw up a statement of the work of the conference for communication to the press at the proper time," Churchill said, and asked the War Cabinet's view of "including in this statement a declaration of the firm intention of the United States and the British Empire to continue the war relentlessly until we have brought about the 'unconditional surrender' of Germany and Japan." See Feis, *ibid.*, 110-111.

[33] *Politics of War*, 291.

which was to provide "for economic reconstruction and expansion of British exports." The "combination of all these things" he spoke of had nothing at all to do with British–American disputes, as Kolko alleged, but instead referred to domestic arguments that probably would be raised against the administration's program.[34]

Kolko's use of documentary materials afforded him several advantages over less imaginative scholars, among them the ability to detect American policies previously unrecognized. Alluding to Washington's efforts to bring the British into line by crippling their export trade, Kolko produced this revelation:

> So far as America was concerned it was not bound to sell to the British goods or materials for the export trade that the War Production Board defined as in "short supply," and it was explicitly understood [Lend-Lease Administrator Leo T.] Crowley would apply this definition in accordance with the true American policy, which Washington kept secret, or permitting only "certain minor British exports prior to V-E Day."[35]

The quotation cited to show what Washington "kept secret" actually pertained only to Lend-Lease items, not, as Kolko has it, to goods the United States sold to Great Britain. It appears in a memo responding favorably to a British request for modifications of Lend-Lease agreements, and reads in full: "Mr. Crowley has stated that he will go as far as practibly possible to make such administrative arrangements, under the terms of the White Paper [a British pledge not to reexport Lend-Lease goods],

[34] *FRUS, 1944* III, 70-74.　　[35] *Politics of War*, 293.

as will not hinder unduly certain minor British exports prior to V-E Day."[36] The "secret" policy, therefore, never existed outside the pages of *The Politics of War*.

Sources having to do with American–Russian relations fared no better in Kolko's hands. Concerning a Russian request for postwar loans, Kolko concluded:

> By this stage of the war there was hardly anyone in Washington who felt that it was to American interests to see a strong Russia emerge from the war, and the idea of aiding it to do so was not at all attractive. [W. Averell] Harriman opposed granting the Russian request, and thought "our basic interests might better be served by increasing our trade with other parts of the world," especially Western Europe.[37]

In context, Harriman's quoted passage occurs in a discussion of "how large a credit we can safely extend to the Soviet Union," and the quotation itself refers to a Treasury Department proposal to give *preferential* treatment to Russia in purchasing from her certain strategic goods for stockpile. Although he was in no position to estimate precisely what amounts of these materials the United States ought to buy from Russia, Harriman said, he added that "our basic interests might better be served by increasing our trade [in these strategic goods alone] with other parts of the world rather than giving preference to the Soviet Union as a source of supply."[38] And he mentioned Brazil, West Africa, and India as alternatives, not Western Europe.

On the matter of reparations from Germany, an im-

[36] *FRUS, 1944* III, 78.   [37] *Politics of War*, 500.
[38] *FRUS, 1945* v, 995.

116

portant source of friction contributing to the deterioration of Russian–American relations, Kolko also employed an interesting procedure. At Potsdam, he wrote, Secretary of State James F. Byrnes repeatedly told the Russians that their zone of occupation contained "one half of Germany's 'existing wealth,' " despite the fact that his aides had "confidentially informed him" that the actual amount was far less. And Kolko cited figures on prewar manufacturing and mining, agricultural resources, and such to make his point.[39] But the very document from which he took his data, a report prepared by Byrnes's aides entitled "Estimated Wealth in U.S.S.R. Zone of Occupation," concluded that the total of specific categories amounted to 49.1%![40] American estimates were misrepresented by Kolko in *The Politics of War* rather than by Byrnes at Potsdam.

Perhaps Kolko's most striking misuse of evidence can be seen in his treatment of American–Russian conflict over the question of Poland's western boundary. Russia, insisting that German territory east of the line formed by the Oder–western Neisse rivers be awarded to Poland, had unilaterally turned over control of the area to the Poles by the time of the Potsdam Conference. There, when Truman refused to sanction this act, he "reneged on clear commitments that the United States made at Yalta 'that Poland must receive substantial accessions of territory in the north and west.' " The President's complaint that he did not see "how reparations or other questions could be decided if Germany was carved up" Kolko dismissed on the ground that the disputed area contained "a maximum of seven percent of Germany's industrial and min-

[39] *Politics of War*, 572. [40] *Potsdam Papers* II, 877.

117

ing output." When the Russians stood firm, "Truman now insisted that the border adjustments were 'a matter for the peace conference,' " but what he did not tell them was that "Washington already had made the decision" that there would be no such conference. The President obstructed settlement, according to Kolko, because "the Americans found it less important to attain equity and stability in Europe than to arrest Russian power in every way possible."[41]

Kolko's account of the situation is bizarre. In refusing to accept the Oder–Neisse line, the United States violated no "clear commitments" made at Yalta or anywhere else. On the contrary, precisely because Roosevelt and Churchill had opposed that boundary at Yalta, the phrase "substantial accessions of territory" was used in place of specific definitions.[42] At Potsdam the United States was prepared ("with reluctance") to support Polish claims up to the Oder River, but not to the western Neisse, which line involved an additional area of 8,100 square miles and a prewar German population of 2.7 million.[43] Kolko's insinuation that anything short of the Oder–Neisse failed to meet the criterion of "substantial accessions" has no basis in fact. And what he neglected to point out was that Russian enthusiasm for the more westerly line had developed only a few weeks before Yalta; throughout 1943 and 1944 Stalin had found the Oder boundary satisfactory compensation for the Poles.[44]

[41] *Politics of War*, 576-579.

[42] *Yalta Papers*, 231-234, 667-671, 716-717, 792-793, 974.

[43] See Briefing Book Paper, "Suggested United States Policy Regarding Poland," *Potsdam Papers* I, 743-747.

[44] Feis, *Churchill-Roosevelt-Stalin*, 521.

Truman's protest about carving up Germany, more-over, pertained only secondarily to the boundary question per se. Ten days before the Potsdam Conference met, Marshal Zhukov had informed the Americans that "any resources east of the Oder Neisse line are not available in the joint administration of German territory."[45] This decision directly violated previous agreements on occupation zones, and Stalin himself admitted at Potsdam that "the Germany of 1937" should be the entity considered for reparations.[46] Kolko mentioned none of this. Nor did he depict accurately the economic consequences of Russia's move, for, in addition to the figure he cited on mining and industrial output, the area turned over to the Poles contained 12 percent of Germany's movable capital assets and "a large part of the food surpluses of Germany."[47] It can be argued that Truman should have accepted Russia's action as a *fait accompli*, but his charge that it had the effect of carving up Germany was perfectly true.

Finally, there is Truman's reference to a peace conference, which Kolko presented as a mere device used to block further negotiations. In fact, the Yalta agreement specifically stated that the "final delimitation of the Western frontier of Poland should thereafter await the Peace Conference."[48] No one at Potsdam suggested otherwise. Stalin himself, just moments before Truman uttered the words Kolko cited, had said that "the final settlement would, of course, be left to the peace conference."[49] For his contention that the United States already had decided

[45] *Potsdam Papers* I, 756.　　[46] *Ibid.* I, 757; II, 90.
[47] *Ibid.* I, 783; II, 842.　　[48] *Yalta Papers*, 905.
[49] *Potsdam Papers* II, 209.

there would be no conference, Kolko put forward no evidence whatever. By placing together misstatements of fact, quotations wrenched out of context, and unsupported allegations, he constructed an entirely misleading version of what actually took place.

Most parts of *The Politics of War* reflect the same standards of scholarship. In making his case that the United States consistently sabotaged the European Advisory Commission, Kolko wrote that in September 1944 Roosevelt "evaluated" it as "a body operating 'on a tertiary and not even a secondary level.' "[50] But that is not what F.D.R. said. Commenting on a specific subject, the treatment of German industry, he stated that the Commission, *"in a case like this,* is on a tertiary and not even a secondary level."[51] Elsewhere Kolko has the American Embassy in Moscow reporting that the Czechoslovakians were " 'expressing deep satisfaction' " over the treatment accorded them by Russia.[52] What the Embassy actually reported was that a *Tass* despatch from London made this claim, which is scarcely the same thing.[53] Concerning America's "shifting policy on the postwar condition of the Far East," Kolko cited a State Department memo on China that "did not once mention the Kuomintang or Chiang" and hoped merely for a government "that would 'safeguard the principle of equal opportunity for the commerce and industry of all nations in China. . . .' "[54] The memo did not mention the Kuomintang or Chiang for the simple reason that its author referred to Chiang's regime

[50] *Politics of War*, 42.
[51] *Yalta Papers*, 155 (emphasis added).
[52] *Politics of War*, 128.
[53] *FRUS, 1944* IV, 870.   [54] *Politics of War*, 530.

as "the Chinese government." And the quotation having to do with "equal opportunity" does not pertain to what was expected of some unspecified future Chinese government, but to what the United States should insist upon from other signatories of the Nine Power Pact of 1922.[55] Similar examples of scholarship gone awry infest the pages of Kolko's book.

In his acknowledgments to those who had aided him in preparing his manuscript, Kolko called special attention to a colleague's "critical commitment to seeking truth . . . ." "Whole sections" of *The Politics of War*, according to its author, were written in response to that commitment. The response, one must conclude, was singularly inappropriate.

[55] *Potsdam Papers* I, 858.

121

6.

YALTA: DIANE SHAVER CLEMENS

Diane Shaver Clemens's *Yalta* is one of the
more recent contributions to revisionist historiography on
the origins of the Cold War.[1] The book appears to have
been written by two different people. The bulk of it, having to do with the Crimean conference itself, is a detailed,
at times penetrating analysis of the negotiations carried
on there. Her conclusions, though often debatable, are
crisply argued and compel one's attention. Her compari-
sons of American and Russian sources are especially
noteworthy. In her final chapter, however, Clemens
abandoned the role of historian for that of prosecutor.
Charging that the United States systematically violated
those of the Yalta accords most crucial to Russian security, she constructed a brief in which she disregarded the
most elementary scholarly procedures. The latter portion
of her work, the subject of this essay, provides a sobering
example of the excesses to which "commitment" can lead.

Clemens's assessment of Rooseveltian diplomacy is
unique among treatments by revisionist scholars. She
denied that Yalta represented the climax of F.D.R.'s consistent effort to build a working partnership with the
Soviet Union or was merely a holding action dictated by
an unfavorable military situation. Rather, to Clemens,
Roosevelt's behavior at Yalta marked a sharp break with
his propensity to postpone hard decisions and with his

[1] (New York: Oxford University Press, 1970.)

previous willingness to ignore Russia's minimum needs. Roosevelt was a moralist, she wrote, with "intermittent periods of realism," and "Yalta was a brief and reasonable interlude rather than a consistent feature of American foreign policy." The decisions reached were equitable to all sides on the whole and represented a triumph for "traditional negotiation" as opposed to unilateral actions. Indeed, Clemens concluded, "it is perhaps relevant to ask what the world would have been like if the spirit of Yalta had triumphed."[2]

The author of *Yalta* hazarded no guess as to what would have happened had Roosevelt lived. His conduct at the conference was atypical, she claimed, for "in Washington and in conversations with his advisers [Roosevelt] demonstrated many of the views and attitudes that found a logical conclusion in the Truman administration."[3] As these words make clear, whatever her doubts about Roosevelt, Clemens entertained none at all about his successor. From the time he assumed office, we are told in *Yalta*, the new President set about destroying the structure of accommodation hammered out during the Crimean conference. Without qualification and without exception, Clemens attributed the origins of the Cold War solely to American actions. Stalin responded as he did because he had no other choice.

Clemens's use of evidence throughout her pages dealing with Truman's alleged violations of the Yalta accords is altogether remarkable. A hint of things to come can be seen in her version of the assumptions under which the new President developed his policies. His overall approach

[2] *Yalta*, 279, 291.   [3] *Ibid.*, 279.

to Russia, she wrote, was formulated on this basis: "Our agreements with the Soviet Union have been a one-way street . . . it was now or never . . . (the Russians) could go to hell."[4] These phrases, it will be recalled, are snippets from a statement Truman made to his advisors on April 23, 1945, just before meeting with Molotov. Alluding to the possibility that Russia would boycott the forthcoming San Francisco Conference if the Polish issue were not resolved to her satisfaction, Truman said "that he felt our agreements with the Soviet Union so far had been a one-way street and that could not continue: it was now or never. He intended to go on with the plans for San Francisco and if the Russians did not wish to join us they could go to hell."[5] Clemens's use of ellipses converted a remark made in a specific context (referring to a specific contingency) into a fundamental statement of policy. And, following the lead of some earlier revisionists, she made it appear that Truman was criticizing the agreements as such, rather than what he considered Russian violations of them.

Having established Truman's contempt for the obligations incurred by Roosevelt, Clemens went on to explore in detail the new President's transgressions. During his conference with Molotov, shortly after Roosevelt's death, Truman insisted that "the Soviet government carry out the Crimea decision on Poland." Yet, according to Clemens, he handed the Russian Minister "a memorandum which equated fulfillment of the Yalta decisions with establishment of a 'new' government." To Clemens this in itself constituted proof of Truman's perfidy, for "at Yalta the

[4] *Ibid.*, 269.   [5] *FRUS, 1945* v, 253.

United States had agreed in writing to a 'reorganized' version of the Polish Provisional Government 'which is now functioning in Poland.' "[6]

Truman's apparent digression from the Yalta agreement has no basis in fact. The Yalta agreement stated:

> *The Provisional Government which is now functioning in Poland should therefore be reorganized* on a broader democratic basis with the inclusion of democratic leaders from Poland itself and from Poles abroad. This *new* government should then be called the Polish Provisional Government of National Unity. [It went on to set up a Commission to preside over consultation among the various Polish leaders.][7]

Truman's note said:

> There was an agreement at Yalta in which President Roosevelt participated for the United States Government, *to reorganize the Provisional Government now functioning in Warsaw* in order to establish a *new* government of National Unity in Poland by means of previous consultation between representatives of the Provisional Polish Government of Warsaw and other Polish democratic leaders from Poland and from abroad.[8]

In brief, Truman's note was merely a paraphrase of the Yalta accord itself. By plucking the word "new" from his message and contrasting it with the word "reorganized" from the Yalta document, Clemens made it seem as though Truman were reneging upon what the United States had agreed to "in writing."

[6] *Yalta*, 269.
[7] *Yalta Papers*, 980 (emphasis added).
[8] *FRUS, 1945* v, 258 (emphasis added).

126

The rest of her analysis of American behavior on the Polish question flowed directly from her contention that Truman violated the Yalta accords within weeks of taking office. He "reverted—briefly"—to them when he sent Harry Hopkins to Moscow at the end of May, but this was merely a delaying tactic. Then, when the United States "was in a stronger position," Truman "at the proper time" insisted on free elections. Although free elections had been provided for at Yalta, this too is presented by Clemens as a provocative act. There "was no reason to believe" that Stalin would not have allowed "moderately" free elections had he not felt threatened, but Western hostility ("everything short of war") forced him to abandon this approach "in favor of consolidation of a defensive perimeter in Eastern Europe."[9] As for Stalin's "record" on free elections, Clemens cited Finland and Austria and Russian noninterference in Western areas, but neglected to mention Bulgaria or Rumania.

The Western hostility Clemens referred to presumably manifested itself in what she presented as Truman's across-the-board betrayal of those parts of the Yalta agreements in which Russia was most interested—reparations, for instance. Although Truman admitted that "morally [Germany] should have been made to pay," according to Clemens, "he decided that 'America was not interested in reparations for anybody.' " Nor was that all, one finds in *Yalta*:

> American hostility toward the Soviet Union was so obvious that Philip Mosely [Political Advisor to the Representative on the European Advisory Commission] had to

[9] *Yalta*, 269-270.

warn the Assistant Secretary of State about it: Moscow might get the impression that the United States sympathized more with the Germans than with the Soviet people by the end of the war.[10]

When read in context, Clemens's "evidence" for her statements has little to do with what she was trying to prove. Truman's remark about America's lack of interest in reparations did not apply to Germany, as she made it appear, but to Italy.[11] And Mosely was not warning anyone about American "hostility." His words pertained to a specific subject: the definition of what constituted "war booty." Because the Soviet Union had been so recently "plundered almost to the last nail and thread," he concluded, the Russians saw "American and British reluctance to see the same treatment meted out to Germany as evidence of greater sympathy for the German people than for the Soviet people." Mosely did not even say that the Russians were correct, merely that their suffering under German occupation had caused them to "have their own set of principles, based on intense popular feeling and fresh experience."[12]

Clemens exhibited the same penchant for inaccuracies in her discussion of negotiations over reparations at Potsdam. Referring to a plan Secretary of State Byrnes put forward, she has Assistant Secretary Will Clayton telling Byrnes "that this 'would be considered by the Russians as

[10] *Ibid.*, 270.

[11] Truman, *Year of Decisions*, 323, 398. "What sum, Stalin asked, was Italy prepared to pay in the form of equipment which might be available? I answered that I would not even venture a guess and that, in any event, America was not interested in reparations for anybody."

[12] *Potsdam Papers* II, 852.

128

a reversal of the Yalta position in Moscow' "—"which indeed it was," Clemens added. This was so because Byrnes insisted "that reparations should come only from the zone under the control of the occupying power," and his plan "effectively denied the Soviet Union access to the industrial goods in the Western zones." As finally drawn, the Potsdam agreement on reparations allowed Russia *only* 15 percent of the capital equipment in the Western zone not necessary for the German peace economy in exchange for raw materials of equivalent value, plus 10 percent of the industrial equipment deemed unnecessary for the German economy."[13]

First of all, Byrnes never insisted that reparations should come "only from the zone under the control of the occupying power." He informed Molotov that "he had in mind working out arrangements for the exchange of needed products between the zones . . . ."[14] Clayton's statement, moreover, did not constitute a criticism of Byrnes's plan, as Clemens made it seem. What Clayton wrote was that he felt "any decision to exclude [the Russians] from any participation in the distribution of the heavy equipment in the Ruhr as reparation, would be considered by the Russians as a reversal of the Yalta and Moscow position . . . ."[15] The point is that the Ruhr lay within the British zone and at that time they had not assented to the Byrnes plan for the exchange of goods. Finally, Clemens neglected to mention that the percentage figures of ("only") 15 and 10 were those put forward by Stalin himself, not Byrnes.[16]

[13] *Yalta*, 271 (emphasis added).
[14] *Potsdam Papers* II, 450.
[15] *Ibid.*, 901.   [16] *Ibid.*, 514-518.

Another of Truman's sins, according to Clemens, was "Washington's reversal of the Yalta decision on German dismemberment." The Soviets accepted this, since they "had never been enthusiastic" about dismemberment in the first place, but it nevertheless constituted a clear-cut violation of the Yalta agreements. Clemens put it this way:

> When the British and American representatives in the European Advisory Council argued that dismemberment "was to be accomplished only as a last resort," the Soviets accepted this position and also came out against dismemberment. The West immediately charged that the Soviet Union was changing its position. Harry Hopkins asked Stalin why he had altered his previous stand. Stalin replied that it was because "both Great Britain and the United States were opposed to dismemberment." Dismemberment disappeared from the military instrument and from the Declaration issued on June 5 by the victorious powers.[17]

Thus, as Clemens has it, the United States not only violated the Yalta accord but then criticized the Soviet Union for accepting the violation. If true, such behavior certainly warranted her allegations of "hostility."

Clemens's account is incorrect in some instances, misleading in others. She neglected to point out, for instance, that the American representative on the Dismemberment Committee (U.S. Ambassador to Great Britain, John G. Winant) reported to Washington that in response to a draft circulated after the first meeting of the committee (on March 7), the Russian member submitted the follow-

[17] *Yalta*, 272.

ing proposal: "Soviet Government understands Crimea Conference decision in respect to Germany's dismemberment not as an obligatory plan for dismemberment but as a possibility for exercising pressure on Germany with aim of rendering Germany harmless in case other means should prove inadequate."[18] Her allegation that the American member of the committee "argued that dismemberment 'was to be accomplished only as a last resort,'" moreover, is not supported by her source—Hopkins's report of his discussions with Stalin. Stalin claimed only that when the British presented their point of view, Winant "interposed no objection."[19] This Stalin took for assent. Actually, Winant did not commit the United States because Roosevelt thought "our attitude should be one of study and postponement of final decision."[20] The fact remains that when Stalin on May 8 proclaimed that "the Soviet Union . . . does not intend to dismember or destroy Germany," he did so unilaterally and without consulting the United States.[21] Clemens's statement that "the West immediately charged that the Soviet Union was changing its position" is false, unless one considers Hopkins's inquiry as such.

The United States consistently violated existing zonal arrangements, according to *Yalta*. Well before the German surrender, Clemens pointed out, Churchill suggested to Truman that Western troops remain within the future Soviet zone as a bargaining chip to force the Russians to provide food from their own zone to the zones of the other powers. Ambassador Winant, she noted, protested

[18] *FRUS, 1945* III, 205-206.
[19] Sherwood, *Roosevelt and Hopkins*, 904.
[20] *FRUS, 1945* III, 221.   [21] *Ibid.*, 317, n. 7.

to Washington that such a move would damage severely the prospects of future cooperation with the Soviet Union.

> Churchill nonetheless insisted on altering the military surrender document because, as he told Eisenhower, he feared that the provisions for joint control gave Stalin a lever to demand Allied troop withdrawal from the Soviet zones. The surrender document was accordingly changed. The Allied Control Council was put on ice. Despite this, Stalin appointed Zhukov as the Soviet delegate to the Council when Hopkins advised him that Eisenhower would represent the United States.

Eisenhower himself "pressured" for the withdrawal of troops from the Soviet zone, Clemens wrote, but the Joint Chiefs of Staff demurred. "Finally on June 12," responding to arguments put forward by Eisenhower and Hopkins and to his fear of a "strong public reaction," Truman notified Churchill: " 'I am unable to delay the withdrawal of American troops from the Soviet zone in order to use pressure in the settlement of other problems.' "[22]

Clemens's narrative is a splendid example of revisionist methodology. She correctly reported Churchill's proposal and Winant's complaint, but omitted mentioning that the United States refused to go along with the British on this matter.[23] Her account of Churchill's role in "altering the military surrender document" is typical. Instead of consulting the relevant documents (available in published form), she based her version on Gar Alperovitz's *Atomic Diplomacy*. Alperovitz, as shown in an earlier

[22] *Yalta*, 272.
[23] *FRUS, 1945* III, 231-232, 235-236, 240. Philip E. Mosely, *The Kremlin and World Politics: Studies in Soviet Policy and Action* (New York: Random House, 1960), 185-186.

chapter, rarely got his facts straight, and in this case he seems to have ignored them entirely: the sources *he* referred to say nothing of the kind.[24] What Clemens meant by her statement that the Control Council "was put on ice" can only be guessed. In fact, the United States wanted the Council to preside over troop withdrawals, while the Soviet Union insisted that it could not begin its functions until the withdrawals had taken place.

The remainder of Clemens's passage on this issue similarly distorted what actually happened. On June 2 Eisenhower cabled the Joint Chiefs of Staff asking that a date be established for troop withdrawals to begin because "it is possible" the Russians would demand such action as a prerequisite to forming the Control Council. The Chiefs of Staff, with Truman's approval, informed Eisenhower on the next day that withdrawals should not be a "condition precedent" to establishing the Control Council on a functioning basis. "As to the actual movement of U. S. forces," the cable read, "its timing will be in accordance with U. S. ability to withdraw their forces from other than their own zone and British and Russian ability to take over."[25] On the 6th, after meeting with Zhukov, Eisenhower notified the Joint Chiefs that his assumption about the Russian position was correct. Eisenhower's recommendation (along with a similar one by his political advisor, Robert D. Murphy) that a firm date for withdrawals

[24] *FRUS, 1945* III, 283-284, 289-290, 294-297. For Alperovitz's version, see *Atomic Diplomacy*, 82-84. Alperovitz cited Mosely's *The Kremlin and World Politics*, Feis's *Between War and Peace*, and Walter Bedell Smith's *My Three Years in Moscow*. None of these sources supports his allegations.

[25] Both cables are reprinted in Truman's *Year of Decisions*, 301.

be set was forwarded by the State Department to Truman on June 8. Harry Hopkins (who had just talked with Eisenhower) supported the General's request.[26] Four days later ("finally," to Clemens) Truman announced his decision to begin troop withdrawals on June 21.[27]

Clemens loaded her case by several significant omissions. First of all, Truman's statement to Churchill that he was unable to delay withdrawal "in order to use pressure in the settlement of other problems" was made in direct response to one of many requests by the Prime Minister that the United States utilize such pressure.[28] By failing to note this, Clemens made it seem as though the President were complaining about what *he* (rather than Churchill) would have liked to have done. This impression Clemens buttressed by asserting that fear of a "strong public reaction" helped push Truman into a decision he would have preferred not to make. Perhaps this was true, but not according to the President. Clemens took the phrase from Eisenhower's cable of June 2, not from anything Truman said or wrote.[29] Finally, she omitted Stalin's response to the President's message informing him of the date set for the withdrawal to begin. "To my regret," Stalin replied, he had to say that the American proposal "meets with certain difficulties . . . ." Mentioning a parade scheduled in Moscow (which would require the presence of Russian commanders then in Germany) and pointing out that "not all the districts of Berlin have been cleared of mines," Stalin requested that Truman delay the begin-

[26] See *FRUS, 1945* III, 328-332, 333-334.
[27] *Ibid.*, 133-134.   [28] *Ibid.*, 132.
[29] Truman, *Year of Decisions*, 301.

ning of troop movements until July 1![30] Stalin, apparently, regarded Truman's "violations" of zonal arrangements far more benignly than did the author of *Yalta*.

But, to Clemens, "the West was not through tampering with the zonal agreement." A zone for the French, she wrote, "as decided earlier, was to be created from the existing American and British zones." In spite of that decision, the British and Americans later proposed "that a French sector be created in Berlin by taking a *Bezirk* [district] from the Soviet section." Philip Mosely, according to Clemens, "found the War Department 'adamant on the question of detaching one *Bezirk* from the Soviet sector in Berlin. The Western commanders had urged the Soviets to continue supplying all of Berlin with food and fuel for the economic needs of Berlin.'" The results of Anglo-American "tampering" were depicted, in *Yalta*, as catastrophic. The Soviet Government protested "angrily to this breach of agreement," complaining that "such a proposal was contrary to Yalta." It directed Zhukov to refuse to supply the Allies with food and went on to "establish the Soviet zone as a separate economic and political area." Ambassador Winant's "warning of the consequences of America's unilateral policy," Clemens wrote, "was borne out": " 'I fear we may cause deep and deplorable discouragement on the British side and indifference on the part of the Russians and thereby jeopardize the chances of obtaining effective Anglo-Russian-American cooperation for the immediate post-war hostilities.' "[31]

Clemens's presentation of this matter is so fanciful as to resist cogent analysis. Occupation zones for Berlin had

[30] *FRUS, 1945* III, 137.   [31] *Yalta*, 273.

not been decided upon at Yalta. The Anglo-American proposal did not, as Clemens made it seem, suggest that the French zone be carved out of the Soviet sector alone. It asked that each of the three powers turn over one *Bezirk* to the French.[32] The Russians did argue that the proposal violated the *intention* of the Yalta agreement on zonal arrangements for the French, but only at first. Later they refused to accept it on the ground that their zone had suffered greater devastation and, hence, that it would be more equitable to create the French zone from the American and British sectors only.[33] The Russian view prevailed in any event, and Clemens's allegation that the British and Americans committed a "breach of agreement" merely by making the proposal was more than a little strained.

Once again, Clemens exhibited a strange inability to transcribe correctly the material in her sources. What Philip Mosely wrote, for instance, was that he found the War Department "at the working level" adamant on the question of detaching a *Bezirk* from the Soviet zone. She omitted entirely from her quotation his very next sentence: "Two days later, however, this point of view was reversed."[34] And her use of Ambassador Winant's "warning" is astonishing. The quotation was taken from a letter Winant wrote on *January 4, 1944*, which had nothing at all to do with zones of occupation.[35] As for her contention that the Soviet decision to establish its zone as "a separate economic and political area" was made as a consequence of the Anglo-American proposal, it is enough to

[32] *FRUS, 1945* III, 352-353.
[33] *Potsdam Papers* I, 598-604.
[34] Mosely, *The Kremlin and World Politics*, 184.
[35] See *FRUS, 1944* I, 3.

say that Clemens read into her source what it did not contain.[36]

What is one to make of such a performance? Scholars rarely agree over the selection and interpretation of the materials they use, nor would it be reasonable to expect them to do otherwise. But whatever latitudes may be justified by "theoretical framework" or "angle of approach," Clemens exceeded them frequently and, at times, grossly. Her citation of Ambassador Winant's letter—written more than a year and a half earlier on a different subject —as though it were a "warning" about American actions on the Berlin question is only the most egregious of a multitude of similar misuses of evidence. That such errors occur so often and, moreover, invariably lend the appearance of substance to her themes renders implausible the explanation of mere carelessness. Perhaps "overzealousness" is the most charitable word one can use to describe her efforts to indict the Truman administration for causing the Cold War.

[36] Her reference is to Mosely's *The Kremlin and World Politics*, 184. But Mosely did not write that the Anglo-American proposal caused the Russians to establish their zone as a separate economic and political area. What he said was that the Russian decision (announced on July 7) not to provide the other zones with food made it seem "undesirable to reduce the size of the Soviet sector. The War Department representatives therefore abandoned their insistence on subtracting one *Bezirk* from the Soviet sector." For evidence that the Russian decision was not made within the context of the Anglo-American proposal, see *Potsdam Papers* I, 630-633.

7.

ARCHITECTS OF ILLUSION:
LLOYD C. GARDNER

L LOYD C. GARDNER's *Architects of Illusion: Men and Ideas in American Foreign Policy, 1941-1949* is the most sophisticated and convincing account of how the Cold War began yet written from the New Left point of view.[1] Wholly lacking in the stridency that characterized previous revisionist works, it is persuasively argued and extremely well-written. One reviewer, in a major historical journal, called it "the most important contribution to the continuing debate on the origins of the Cold War."[2] It is also, one must add, a compendium of myths invented by earlier revisionist writers, and it contains as well an impressive number developed by Gardner himself.

Gardner's thesis closely resembles that of William Appleman Williams, though with certain modifications. American policymakers during World War II, according to *Architects of Illusion*, were convinced that the nation's domestic well-being following the conflict would depend upon the existence of a liberal world order based on multilateral trade and investment (Williams's "Open Door"). Haunted by the specter of another depression, they were committed to securing such a world system as the only alternative to the imposition of comprehensive controls

[1] (Chicago: Quadrangle, 1970.)

[2] George C. Herring, Jr., *The Journal of American History* LVII (December 1970), 756.

over the American economy. Their assumptions led them to oppose the creation of blocs or spheres of influence anywhere in the world (excepting our own in Latin America) and brought the United States into conflict with both Great Britain and the Soviet Union. The British had to bow before most American demands, albeit reluctantly. But Russia defined her security as requiring a sphere of influence in Eastern Europe whatever the costs, and she refused to retreat despite American economic diplomacy and, at war's end, possession of the atomic bomb. The illusion American leaders held was that they could somehow achieve the traditional goals of a liberal world order in the face of existing power realities. "Responsibility for the *way* in which the Cold War developed, at least," Gardner therefore concluded, "belongs more to the United States."[3]

Unlike Williams, Gardner did not try to argue that American economic interests in Eastern Europe were of any great moment. "If Eastern Europe had been the only issue . . . ," he wrote, "there probably would have been no Cold War." Instead, that region became "the locus of a broader conflict" involving spheres of influence in all of Europe and Asia.[4] "Economic opportunity in Eastern Europe was not essential to American capitalists," as he put it, "but an open world was—especially after twelve years of depression and war."[5] And, according to Gardner, American leaders perceived that Soviet expansion, "even if limited to countries geographically close to Russia, was a potential threat to the next 'tier' of states in Central Europe." This last point approximates the "orthodox"

[3] *Architects of Illusion*, 317.   [4] *Ibid.*, ix.
[5] *Ibid.*, 319.

140

view, except for Gardner's contention that American policymakers opposed such expansion almost exclusively for
economic reasons. "The more states Russia fenced in behind the 'Iron Curtain,'" he wrote, "the more likely it
would be that the American economy would be forced to
the left."[6]

Believing as he did that American foreign policies reflected a near-consensus among top officials over the needs
of the domestic economy, Gardner did not perceive any
sharp break in diplomacy when Truman succeeded Roosevelt as President. The only real difference, apart from
personal styles, was that whereas Roosevelt had followed
a "complicated strategy of postponement" during the war,
Truman had to grapple with the contradictions inherent
in his predecessor's "defense of traditional American objectives and the requirements of an effective coalition in
peacetime as well as in war."[7] In short, Truman had to
pay the bills. Without saying so explicitly, Gardner strongly suggested that the logic of Rooseveltian diplomacy
made it unlikely that the course of U.S. relations with the
Soviet Union would have run very differently had F.D.R.
lived a year or two longer.

Portions of the hypotuesis put forward in *Architects of
Illusion* are easily verified. American leaders did oppose
spheres of influence (Latin America excepted) and political or economic blocs, believing as they did that such
arrangements had contributed directly to the outbreak of
both world wars. They also favored the growth of American trade and investment as a general principle—if there
were any officials who wished to have the United States
excluded from particular regions, they refrained from ex-

[6] *Ibid.*, 72.   [7] *Ibid.*, 56.

pressing such views openly. Finally, many Americans in and outside the government voiced apprehension over the possibility of a postwar depression. What Gardner failed to demonstrate convincingly was the relationship these attitudes had to American foreign policy, particularly with reference to the origins of the Cold War.

The basic weakness of *Architects of Illusion* is Gardner's inability to provide any real evidence that the men actually charged with the conduct of American diplomacy acted out of the motives and assumptions he attributed to them. If, for instance, American policies toward Eastern Europe were dictated by the fear of depression and a shift to the left (even accepting Gardner's qualification that Eastern Europe was seen as but part of a larger struggle), one would expect to find those who made policy discussing the issues in such a related way with each other, if not publicly. Gardner was unable to show that any such discussions ever took place. His efforts to deflect attention from this most crucial gap in his argument were ingenious, but they cannot withstand analysis.

One of the practices Gardner most commonly employed was to attribute to American policymakers certain conceptions, the proof for which consisted of statements made by people other than those about whom he was writing. A typical example can be seen in his effort to show that Truman went to Potsdam determined to open up Eastern Europe (and other areas) as a means of staving off a move to the left at home. Gardner quoted in support of this contention Herbert Hoover, Alfred M. Landon, and Eugene V. Rostow, the latter identified as "a student of the Russian political-economic system and future State Department planner." Then, he concluded, "as

142

these comments make clear, the real issue was not preservation of Eastern Europe markets but the preservation
and extension of a trade system among all nations (if possible) which would enable the United States to keep government intervention to a minimum."[8] In point of fact,
none of the statements he cited referred to the prospects
of increased "government intervention." Even if they had,
however, the result would have been to show what Hoover, Landon, and Rostow thought was the "real issue,"
not what Truman thought it was.

Gardner demonstrated even greater resourcefulness
elsewhere in his book. Seizing upon a statement in Truman's *Memoirs* that "Russian foreign policy was based on
the conclusion that we were heading for a major depression . . . ," he used this to show that Truman's thoughts
were dominated by *his* fears of a depression. The President, according to *Architects of Illusion,* "projected
American economic concern onto Russian minds." Efforts on the part of the United States to keep "the door
open in Eastern Europe" reflected this concern.

> Truman clearly saw it not only as an international ques-
> tion but as a domestic one. Without a functioning world
> system, depression was inevitable. The belief that Rus-
> sia was counting on an American downturn to further
> its own goals was the natural result of such a preoccu-
> pation. . . .[9]

Gardner's foray into the field of psychology would be
worth considering provided Truman's estimate of Russian
assumptions rested upon no basis other than the working
of his own mind. But it did not. In January 1945, when

---

[8] *Ibid.*, 71-72.   [9] *Ibid.*, 56, 57.

the Soviets requested a large postwar loan, they professed to have as their real purpose the wish to help tide the United States through its postwar difficulties.[10] In April Ambassador Harriman told Truman personally that "some quarters in Moscow believed erroneously that American business needed as a matter of life and death the development of exports to Russia."[11] Harriman may have been wrong, but that is another matter. At San Francisco the Ukrainian delegate had made a speech in which he urged the expansion of Russian–American trade as a means of solving "America's unemployment problem." And finally, just before the Potsdam Conference began, Harriman reported that the Soviet press was full of stories along this line; "threat of postwar business crisis and mass unemployment in America was emphasized at every opportunity . . . ."[12] Truman may have misread the Soviet outlook, but it is erroneous to say that his view was based upon nothing more tangible than his own "preoccupation." The facts point toward the conclusion that Gardner projected *his* preoccupation onto Truman's mind.

If the lack of hard evidence caused his broader thesis to suffer from malnutrition, Gardner's handling of specific issues and events produced actual deformities. In some places he simply repeated the errors first put forward by earlier revisionists, even though his own research into pri-

[10] *FRUS, 1945* v, 942. "Having in mind the repeated statements of American figures concerning the desirability of receiving extensive large Soviet orders for the postwar and transition period," said the Russian *aide-mémoire*, "the Soviet Government *considers it possible* to place orders on the basis of long term credits to the amount of six billion dollars" (emphasis added).

[11] *Ibid.*, 232.   [12] *Ibid.*, 866.

mary and secondary sources should have kept him from
going astray. Six representative samples follow:

1. That when Secretary of State James F. Byrnes first
saw "the original Russian request for a multi-billion
dollar credit, he had it placed, he recalled in 1958,
'in the Forgotten File.'" That is false. Byrnes was
referring to a Treasury Department memorandum
calling for a larger loan at a lower interest rate than
the Russians themselves had requested.[13]

2. That Molotov revealed the true implications of
the reparations plan Byrnes proposed at Potsdam in
this exchange:

MR. MOLOTOV: said that would not the Secretary's suggestion mean that each country would
have a free hand in their own zone and would act
entirely independently of the others?

THE SECRETARY: said that was true in substance.

What Byrnes actually said was "that was true in substance but he had in mind working out arrangements
for the exchange of needed products between zones,

[13] *Architects of Illusion*, 87. See Byrnes, *All in One Lifetime*,
310: "It was interesting that the Treasury proposal was submitted
shortly after the Russians had requested that we extend them a
credit of the smaller sum of six billion dollars at the slightly
higher interest rate of two and three-eighth percent. This would
indicate that our Treasury officials were not always the cold-
hearted, glassy-eyed individuals all bankers are supposed to be.
When the memorandum was brought to my attention, I had it
placed in the 'Forgotten File,' as I felt sure that Fred Vinson, the
new Secretary of the Treasury, would not press it."

for example, from the Ruhr if the British agreed, machinery and equipment could be removed and exchanged with the Soviet authorities for goods—food and coal—in the Soviet zone." The latter part of the Secretary's statement undercut the point Gardner was trying to make.[14]

3. That the Western Allies, maneuvering for "important concessions," failed to carry out in good faith the Yalta accord on Poland's western boundary by refusing to recognize the Oder–Neisse line unilaterally established by Russia. As Gardner put it:

> At Yalta it had been agreed that Poland should be compensated in the west for its forced cession of territory to Russia. Great Britain and the United States had since refused to draw a specific boundary, insisting that such things could be decided only at the final peace conference.

Actually, both Churchill and Roosevelt had refused at Yalta to accept the Oder–Neisse line, and the agreement reached stated "that the final delimitation of the western frontier of Poland should thereafter await the Peace Conference." Russia violated the Yalta accord on this matter, not the United States or Great Britain.[15]

4. That when F.D.R. issued the "Unconditional Surrender" statement at the Casablanca Conference, it was to Churchill's "complete surprise." This old chestnut, resurrected by Gabriel Kolko in *The Poli-*

[14] *Architects of Illusion*, 243. See *Potsdam Papers* II, 450.
[15] *Architects of Illlusion*, 74-75. See *Yalta Papers*, 980.

LLOYD C. GARDNER

tics of War, was shown to be false well over a decade ago.[16]

5. That when J. F. Byrnes told President Truman that the atomic bomb "might well put us in a position to dictate our own terms at the end of the war," he was referring to relations with Russia. Gardner's source for this quotation, Truman's *Memoirs,* permits no doubt that Byrnes's remark was made in the context of dictating terms to Japan, not to Russia.[17]

6. That Truman reneged on the Yalta agreement over the makeup of the Polish government because he "demanded not merely a reorganization of the Lublin government but a 'new' provisional government . . . ." But Truman did ask for a reorganization of the Lublin government, and the Yalta agreement itself referred to a "new" provisional government no less than three times in the space of a few short paragraphs.[18]

In other places Gardner reasserted interpretations put forward by earlier revisionists, but substantiated them by different means. The curtailment of Lend-Lease aid in May 1945 provides a case in point. This step was presented in *Architects of Illusion* as one aspect of the "economic diplomacy" Washington employed to coerce the Soviet Union. Like most New Leftists, Gardner omitted

[16] *Architects of Illusion,* 37. See John L. Chase, "Unconditional Surrender Reconsidered," *Political Science Quarterly* LXX (June 1955), 258-279; and Feis, *Churchill-Roosevelt-Stalin,* 108-110.

[17] *Architects of Illusion,* 181. Truman, *Year of Decisions,* 87.

[18] *Architects of Illusion,* 61. See Truman, *Year of Decisions,* 80-81; and *Yalta Papers,* 980.

several crucial facts bearing upon American actions: the reductions applied to all recipients, not just to the Soviet Union; administration leaders all along had interpreted the Lend-Lease Act as affording no legislative basis for continuing shipments intended solely for use in the European theater after the end of hostilities there (Russia was not then at war with Japan); and they had so informed Soviet officials repeatedly.[19] Gardner's "evidence" for his assertion, however, is unique. Although Truman later denied personal responsibility for the abrupt way curtailment was accomplished, he wrote, the President at the time "carefully allowed newsmen a hint of the idea; the administration would handle future aid to the Soviet Union 'in a way which we think will be all right for the peace of the world.'"[20] To construe Truman's remark as an admission that the curtailment of Lend Lease was intended to coerce Russia required an impressive leap of the imagination, particularly when read in context. At the time Truman spoke (in late May), the existing Lend-Lease protocol with the Soviet Union had one more month to run. A reporter asked the President what would happen when it expired. Since Russia had not yet declared war on Japan, and since negotiations over a new protocol were then in progress, Truman refused to answer definitely. What he said was: "Well, let's wait and see what is necessary to be done at that time, then we will take care of it in a way which we think will be all right for the peace of the world."[21]

[19] *FRUS, 1945* v, 954-956, 991-993, 1008-1009, 1018-1021.
[20] *Architects of Illusion*, 66.
[21] Harry S Truman, *Public Papers, 1945* (Washington: Government Printing Office, 1961), 68.

In fine, what to Gardner was a "hint of the idea" ("carefully allowed") was in fact the usual boilerplate public officials dispense in lieu of specific information.

But *Architects of Illusion* is more than a mere refurbishment of existing revisionist legendry. Gardner made significant contributions himself. As pointed out earlier in connection with Poland's western boundary and the makeup of her provisional government, he persistently misrepresented what happened at the Yalta Conference. Consider, for instance, this statement: "While F.D.R. did insist at this plenary session that there be free elections as soon as possible in Poland, the final protocol of the Yalta Conference stated only that the new Polish provisional government should be a 'reorganization' of the Lublin government."[22] That is not what the protocol "only" stated. "This Polish Provisional Government of National Unity," it reads, "shall be pledged to the holding of free and unfettered elections as soon as possible on the basis of universal suffrage and secret ballot."[23]

Throughout the pages of *Architects of Illusion* Gardner placed considerable emphasis upon contemporary magazine articles and editorials, particularly those appearing in journals identified with the world of business. Indeed, he seemed to work under the impression that to cite the opinions of contributors to *Business Week* or *Fortune* was to identify without corroboration the opinions of American policymakers at any given time. Even within this questionable framework Gardner often misconstrued what it was the magazine actually contained. And every one of these misconstructions bolstered his arguments.

The simplest examples of this tendency can be found

---

[22] *Architects of Illusion,* 52.   [23] *Yalta Papers,* 980.

in those instances where Gardner braided into his own prose quotations which appear to substantiate the point he was making but which, when read in context, fail to do so. The following is typical:

> Only with Russia "playing her part," said *Fortune*, was there hope for the future of an open *economic order*.[24]

What *Fortune* actually said was:

> For only with Russia playing her part within an *international order* is there hope for the future.[25]

The statement referred to Russia's political actions within the framework of the United Nations. Gardner's version lent a spurious authenticity to his thesis about the role economics played in American thinking.

Elsewhere Gardner produced more complex variations, as in the following passage:

> In January 1945, *Fortune* magazine's survey of American opinion revealed that 68.2 percent of those queried believed that unemployment would be the most important issue after the war; 48.9 percent also believed there would be a serious depression within ten years. After the Potsdam Conference, 58.9 percent still felt that unemployment was the most important domestic question, but 55.6 percent now thought Russia was an even larger problem. The more Washington pressed the Soviets, the more adamant they became about maintaining their sphere of influence in Eastern Europe, and the bigger the problem looked to the public.[26]

[24] *Architects of Illusion*, 58 (emphasis added).
[25] "Does Russia Want Credit?" *Fortune* XXXII (July 1945), 110 (emphasis added).
[26] *Architects of Illusion*, 57-58.

150

A more misleading comparison of the polls and what they signified would be difficult to imagine. In January the people surveyed were presented a list of issues and asked to rank them according to their importance. Gardner correctly stated that 68.2 percent chose unemployment. *There was no question pertaining to relations with Russia on the list.*[27] The second poll, which appeared in *Fortune*'s August issue, cited four issues, and the question asked was "Which of the things on this list do you think are going to be troublesome problems for this country in the next few years?"[28] Respondents were not asked to rank the issues in order of importance. Gardner's conclusion that concern over Russia had mushroomed following the Potsdam Conference, and that "55.6 percent now thought Russia was an even larger problem [than unemployment]," is false even on its face. What is more, the second poll could not have reflected attitudes toward the Potsdam Conference ("The more Washington pressed the Soviets . . .") for the simple reason that the August issue of *Fortune* had already been printed. Indeed, the September issue of the magazine was in press by the time the meeting ended.[29]

Gardner displayed similar tendencies in using his other sources. An important part of his overall thesis is the American position on reparations from Germany. Lend-Lease curtailment and the failure to grant Russia a large loan were the earliest manifestations of American economic diplomacy, but these measures contained a "hitch," as he put it. Russia might get the wherewithal to finance

[27] "Fortune Survey," *Fortune* XXXII (January 1945), 260ff.
[28] *Ibid.* (August 1945), 257.
[29] "Fortune's Wheels," *Fortune* XXXII (September 1945), 2.

her own reconstruction from Germany, thereby reducing Soviet dependence upon the United States and at the same time strengthening "economic ties between Russia and Germany." Truman moved to forestall that possibility when he "made one more effort before the Potsdam Conference to use 'carrot' diplomacy on the Kremlin." His vehicle was a "new statement" on American reparations policy:

> It remained fundamental to United States policy, said the pronouncement, that German war potential must be destroyed to the extent of leaving no possibility for its future reconstruction. The United States therefore opposed "any reparation plan based on the assumption that . . . [it] or any other country will finance directly or indirectly any reconstruction in Germany or reparation by Germany."

Its implications, to Gardner, were all too clear:

> In the context of Russian–American disputes over Poland and Eastern Europe during May and June, the pronouncement's change in emphasis hinted that the United States was preparing to take a tough stand on all reparations not directly related to the narrowly defined destruction of German war potential. By denying Russia economic aid, first from United States sources, then from German resources, Truman might be able to undo the hitch in economic diplomacy at the same time he kept Germany and Russia apart.[30]

To begin with, Gardner's assertions about what Truman was trying to accomplish are entirely unsupported by evidence—and no wonder. In writing that the Presi-

[30] *Architects of Illusion*, 67-68.

dent's "new statement" appeared "before Potsdam" and in the context of Russian–American disputes "during May and June," he made it seem as though the document were issued in late June or early July as an attempt to "undo the hitch" in previous economic diplomacy. That is incorrect. Truman first approved the paper on *May 10*, virtually the same day that Lend-Lease curtailment was announced.[31] Prepared by a committee, the document was written even earlier and could hardly have represented an attempt to undo hitches in that which had not yet been tried.

Gardner misrepresented the document's nature as well as its timing. By referring to it as a "new statement" and a "pronouncement," he made it appear to be some kind of public announcement which Truman hoped would convince the Soviets to back off in Eastern Europe rather than face the prospect of being denied vitally needed reparations from Germany. This, too, is false. The paper was put together to establish guidelines for American reparations policies and was conveyed privately as instructions to the American representative on the Reparations Commission, Edwin W. Pauley.[32] The Russians could scarcely be expected to perceive "hints" in statements they never saw.

Consistent throughout on this matter, Gardner also distorted what the document actually said. In his version, it stated "that German war potential must be destroyed *to the extent* of leaving no possibility for its future reconstruction." This, presumably, should have been read by the Russians to mean "*only* to the extent," and together

[31] *FRUS, 1945* III, 1222, n. 6.
[32] *Ibid.*, 1222-1227.

with the proviso that the United States would not finance reparations or reconstruction, should have conveyed to them the "hint" that the United States would oppose reparations "not directly related to the narrowly defined destruction of German war potential." But the paper itself reads: "It is and has been fundamental United States policy that Germany's war potential be destroyed, and its resurgence as far as possible be prevented, by removal or destruction of German plants, equipment and other property."[33] There is no suggestion here that the United States meant to limit reparations "to the narrowly defined destruction of German war potential." Indeed, the paragraph quoted above is point number two in the paper: point number one stated that the purpose of the Reparations Commission was to formulate a program whereby Germany would "pay in kind for the losses caused by her to the Allied Nations in the course of the war." And the statement that the United States would not finance German reconstruction or reparations (a consistent policy established well before Yalta) was preceded by this paragraph: "The Reparation Plan should aid in strengthening and developing on a sound basis the industries and trade of the devastated non-enemy countries of Europe and of other United Nations, and in raising the living standards of these countries."[34] Gardner's version of "carrot diplomacy," therefore, is fictitious in every respect: timing, form, *and* content.

Examples of quotations either taken out of context or placed in the wrong temporal sequence occur with depressing frequency in *Architects of Illusion*. Referring to the period immediately prior to the Yalta Conference,

[33] *Ibid.*, 1222.   [34] *Ibid.*

154

Gardner portrayed Roosevelt as feeling trapped between Russian actions in Poland (Russia recognized the Lublin Government on January 1, 1945) and the State Department's insistence "upon the creation of a commission to see that it [the Atlantic Charter] was in fact carried out." "As these pressures mounted," according to Gardner, "Roosevelt's temper flared up at Ambassador-designate to Poland Arthur Bliss Lane, who told him to get tough with the Russians. 'Do you want me to go to war with Russia?' F.D.R. snapped."[35] If true, this would make a telling vignette. But Gardner's source, Lane's *I Saw Poland Betrayed*, states specifically that the meeting during which Roosevelt made the remark took place *in November 1944.*[36]

A bit later, in *Architects of Illusion*, Gardner has Secretary of State Byrnes during the weeks after V-J Day trying to call a general peace conference in order to facilitate American penetration of Eastern Europe:

> The essential precondition for a functioning economic diplomacy—or any other kind of policy—was assured access to the whole area. It was unlikely that this could be accomplished without a large peace conference. The problem was how to get Russia to the table. Once that was accomplished—if it could be—Byrnes was optimistic that the Russians could be "forced by world opinion to co-operate." That proved not to be the fact, but probably not for the reasons Byrnes's critics have put forth.[37]

But Byrnes's remark, in context, did not pertain to calling a peace conference so as to force Russia to cooperate in

[35] *Architects of Illusion*, 49.
[36] (New York: Bobbs-Merrill, 1948), 66.
[37] *Architects of Illusion*, 87-88.

ensuring "access to the whole area" of Eastern Europe. The phrase, taken from his *Speaking Frankly,* was merely part of a general observation he made about Russian behavior at the time the book was written (1947): "Their shift toward collective action within the United Nations is slow and grudging; it is still in progress, but it will continue only so long as and only to the extent that the Soviets are *forced by world opinion to co-operate.*"[38]

Gardner similarly abused his source at the close of his chapter on Harry Truman. The President, according to Gardner, had gained "new confidence" from American possession of the atomic bomb. He expressed that confidence on Navy Day, October 27, 1945, when he christened the new aircraft carrier *USS Franklin D. Roosevelt.* After telling his audience that the United States "would still be the greatest naval power on earth" even after demobilization, Truman went on to explain, as Gardner put it, that

> such power was still needed to fulfill the objectives of American foreign policy. These objectives included refusal to recognize any government imposed upon any nation by a foreign power; the establishment not only of freedom of the seas but of equal rights to the navigation of boundary rivers and waterways passing through more than one country; the protection of the Western Hemisphere states from outside interference; and the cooperation of all states, great and small, in the restoration of the world economy.[39]

This speech, as presented in *Architects of Illusion,* was militant, to say the least, and could have been directed

[38] Byrnes, *Speaking Frankly,* 105 (emphasis added).
[39] *Architects of Illusion,* 83.

toward only one nation—Russia. Economic diplomacy had failed to secure American objectives thus far and now, buoyed by possession of the A-bomb, the President indicated his willingness to employ the threat of military force. In reality, however, Truman did no such thing.

Unimportant in itself but characteristic of Gardner's work is the fact that the speech to which he referred was made on October 27, 1945, but not at the christening of the *Roosevelt*.[40] The President's words on that occasion were given over almost entirely to praise for F.D.R. and to repeated promises that the United States meant to work for peace within the United Nations. A small error, but the image of Truman rattling his sword beneath the prow of an aircraft carrier added a convincing touch to the impression Gardner sought to convey.

Turning to the address in question, one finds Gardner's version of it more than a little misleading. Truman did not say that military power was needed to fulfill the objectives listed in *Architects of Illusion*. He said it was needed to "enforce the terms of peace imposed upon our defeated enemies," to carry out "the military obligations which we are undertaking as a member of the United Nations Organization," to "preserve the territorial integrity and the political independence of the nations of the Western Hemisphere," and to "discharge the fundamental mission laid upon them [the military forces] by the Constitution of the United States—to 'provide for the common defense' of the United States."

The list of objectives from which Gardner extracted the ones he cited were presented later in the speech as "the fundamentals" of American foreign policy. But the

[40] Truman, *Public Papers, 1945*, 428-430.

context within which Truman enumerated these points was the need for the American public to remain patient during the efforts to put them into practice because "we recognize that we have to operate in an imperfect world." After all, as he put it, "the Ten Commandments themselves have not yet been universally achieved over these thousands of years." He stressed the theme of forbearance throughout his talk, as well as the need "to understand the special problems of other nations." "We must seek to understand," he said, "their own legitimate urge towards security as they see it." Far from throwing down the gauntlet to the Soviet Union, Truman was warning the American people against becoming disillusioned, against losing faith "in the effectiveness of international cooperation."[41] By juxtaposing items from the list of "fundamentals" with the President's earlier statement about the need for military power, Gardner seriously distorted the tenor of Truman's speech.

Subtler and more persuasive than previous revisionist works, *Architects of Illusion* in the last analysis rests upon similar foundations. It is history by irrelevant evidence, misused quotations, jumbled figures, and distortions of documentary materials. Gardner is a capable historian; his abilities are apparent throughout the pages of his book. That he squandered his gifts as he did is most unfortunate for those seeking a better understanding of the past. *Architects of Illusion* is a fitting title for a book that is in many ways itself based on illusion.

[41] *Ibid.*, 431-438.

CONCLUSION

IN *Historians' Fallacies* David Hackett Fischer tells
the apocryphal story of a scientist who published an astonishing generalization about the behavior of rats. A doubt-
ing colleague visited his laboratory and asked to see the
records of the experiments upon which the generalization
was based. "Here they are," said the scientist, producing
a notebook from his desk. And pointing to a cage in the
corner, he added, "there's the rat." Fischer used the story
to illustrate the danger involved in developing broad the-
ories from isolated facts. But it offers another lesson as
well. An examination of the *manner* in which new interpretations are reached ought to precede dialogues over
the interpretations themselves. Historians, unfortunately,
seem unwilling to follow this rudimentary procedure.

That a group of individuals should indulge in the practices detailed in preceding pages is, of course, lamentable,
particularly when their works are presented in the guise
of scholarly analyses (some are almost overburdened with
academic paraphernalia), rather than as the polemics
they really are. Perhaps these volumes will be defended
on the ground that there is a higher truth that transcends
factual accuracy, or that such distortions are necessary
to proselytize for desired social and economic goals. It
is certain that these "bold" and "provocative" interpretations have earned fame and academic advancement for
their authors.

And what of the publishers of these books? Did the

159

scholars from whom they solicited advice before agreeing to publish these books fail to report the methods employed in them? Or were their complaints disregarded on the ground that these volumes were "controversial," hence eminently salable? The name of a reputable publisher traditionally has served as a kind of imprimatur for scholarly treatises. It certifies neither interpretation nor approach, but serves rather to assure the reader that the material has been subjected to (and passed) rigorous critical examination. That assumption may no longer be warranted.

Of greater moment, and sadder still, is the fact that experts in diplomatic history, writing in influential journals, have failed to call attention to such practices. In so failing, their reviews have had the effect of endorsing these revisionist works as responsible pieces of historical research, their disagreements with specific interpretations notwithstanding. Scholars, students, and lay readers alike have been poorly served by what can only be regarded as a striking malfunctioning of the critical mechanisms within the historical profession.

"Orthodox" reviews of revisionist books have tended to follow a pattern. The critic begins by praising the work in question as an important contribution to the historical literature on the origins of the Cold War. Phrases such as "calls into question the conventional wisdom" and "raises issues previous studies have ignored" are standard. Then, after a description of the book's theses, a few caveats are entered: "overemphasis," "selective use of evidence," and "rides his theme too hard" are likely to be encountered here. The review ends with a statement to the effect that, despite certain reservations, the book is required reading for anyone interested in the subject. Reviewers who have been known to pounce with scarcely disguised glee on some poor wretch who incorrectly transcribed a middle initial or date of birth have shown a most extraordinary reluctance to expose even the most obvious New Left fictions.

How is one to account for this uncustomary deference? The first possibility, of course, is that some of the reviewers to whom these books were assigned were themselves insufficiently familiar with the historical sources to detect any discrepancies. The second possibility—far more intriguing—is that reviewers who were perfectly aware of the procedures employed nevertheless concluded that it was unnecessary to share this information with their readers. Their motives, like those of the revisionists themselves, can only be surmised. On this question, perhaps, the writer's personal experiences can shed some light.

Preliminary versions of the chapters contained in this work were sent to a number of leading scholars in the field of diplomatic history. Two were sent to scholarly journals and readers' reports were received on both. Overall the response was gratifying, the suggestions helpful. Many of the respondents commented on the desirability of making the material contained available to the widest possible audience. There was dissent from those who thought this type of work ought not to be published. Their reasoning fell into two broad categories, neither of which had anything to do with the accuracy of the analyses themselves.

The first group consisted of those who believed that critiques centering on factual matters were irrelevant to "the basic historiographical issue" between revisionist and

161

orthodox historians. That issue, as one individual put it, "is whether or not ideas or institutions are the controlling factor in historical development." One should not approach revisionist works, therefore, with the object of comparing their conclusions with the evidence upon which the conclusions are presumed to rest. "If one wants to challenge ————," the letter continued, "then challenge him on his basic assumptions about the nature of American institutions and how policies are formulated and for what end, not on whether he was correct on . . . [the material contained in the essay]." On analogy with the story of the scientist and the rat, we might interpret this response by saying that some scholars would not have dreamed of examining either the experiments or the subject of those experiments. Instead, they would have engaged the scientist in a debate over his "basic assumptions about the nature" of rodents.

Historians of the second type exhibited relatively little concern over accuracy *or* relevance. Their complaints had to do with the matter of taste. Without questioning the validity of the charges substantiated in the essays, they expressed reservations over the propriety of publishing them. Or, if it were necessary, some of them said, could not the prose be reworked so as to present each example as a random "mistake," one of those howlers that inevitably creep into the most carefully prepared manuscript? As it was, according to one letter, the argument "comes close to suggesting that ———— consciously compromises his scholarly obligations in his efforts to argue his thesis." The question, then, was not whether ———— did compromise his scholarly obligations, but whether one ought to call attention to the possibility of it. Individuals of this

162

bent, on the grounds of delicacy alone, apparently would have remained silent about the scientist, the experiments, and the rat.

Whatever the reasons, those critics who have permitted revisionist methodologies to go unchallenged have failed to perform an essential task. It is one thing when an individual scholar strains the evidence a bit in order to exaggerate the importance of some obscure politician or general. It is quite another when a growing body of academic historians consistently misuses the fundamental sources of a crucial era in American history. At the very least one must ask to what extent their performances on the matter of the Cold War's origins are characteristic of New Left writing on American foreign policy in general.

The results are already observable. In a survey conducted in 1971, history professors were asked to name those books which had had the greatest effect on students "sharply critical of contemporary U.S. foreign policy."[1] The authors cited most frequently were William Appleman Williams (mentioned nearly twice as often as anyone else), Gabriel Kolko, Gar Alperovitz, and David Horowitz. Excerpts from their books have appeared in some of the most widely used anthologies, especially in those constructed so as to exemplify "conflicting interpretations." Editors, like the book reviewers, thus far have refrained from pointing out even the most obvious distortions these excerpts contain. The result is that students (or any other readers) who do not consult—or have access to—the doc-

[1] "*The New Empire* and American Historians: A Report on a Survey," a paper delivered by Robert L. Beisner at a meeting of the Organization of American Historians, New Orleans, Louisiana, April 16, 1971.

163

uments have no way of distinguishing between those interpretations based upon the evidence as it exists and those based upon the evidence as presented by the revisionists. The difference is crucial. There is every reason to be "sharply critical" of recent American foreign policy, but the criticisms should rest on more substantial foundations.

A New Left version of the origins of the Cold War may be perfectly valid. If so, it remains to be written. Possibly the seven authors whose works were examined in these pages would have been able to document their theses by less exotic techniques had they pursued their research more diligently, or had they been more perceptive in their handling of the materials they did consult. But the range of sources listed in their footnotes and bibliographies appears to belie the former possibility, and their capacity for perceiving support in documents containing none, the latter. Perhaps, after all, the New Left view of American foreign policy during and immediately after World War II can *only* be sustained by doing violence to the historical record?

INDEX

Allied Control Commission, 132-133

Alperovitz, Gar, 54n, 63-78, 132-133, 163

Architects of Illusion, see Gardner, Lloyd C.

Ardennes, battle of, 106-107

Argentina, 88-90

Atlantic Charter, 155

atomic bomb, 4, 20, 22, 23, 31-34, 40, 51-56, 64-65, 68, 69, 70, 75, 76, 140, 146, 156, 157

Atomic Diplomacy, see Alperovitz, Gar

Austria, 127

Beisner, Robert L., 163n

Belgium, 105

Berle, A. A., Jr., 13n

Berlin, zonal arrangements in, 135-137

Bern, meeting of, 83

Bevin, Ernest, 26

Bidault, Georges, 76

Blackett, P.M.S., 65n

Bohlen, Charles E., 65, 66, 94, 95

Bulgaria, 18, 21, 57, 73, 77n, 127

Business Week, 149

Byrnes, James F., 8, 49, 68, 76, 155-156; and German reparations, 21-28, 117, 128-129, 145-146; postwar loan to Russia, 31-32, 145; Russian entry into Far Eastern war, 55-56, 75, 100-101

Casablanca Conference, 113, 146

Chiang Kai-shek, 53, 54, 120-121

China, 33, 53, 55, 56

Churchill, Winston S., 35, 42, 48, 70n, 72, 84, 105, 106, 110, 113, 131-134, 146-147

Clayton, Will, 23, 24, 128-129

Clemens, Diane Shaver, 123-137

Cold War and Its Origins, see Fleming, D. F.

Compton, James V., 5n, 7n

Council of Foreign Ministers, 21, 51

Crowley, Leo T., 115

Czechoslovakia, 18, 120

Deane, John R., 67

de Gaulle, Charles, 76

Eastern Europe, 5, 8, 16, 17, 19, 20, 23, 28, 29, 32, 40, 64, 66, 73-74, 76, 127, 140, 142-143, 150, 152, 153

165